OCLC RESEARCH REPORT

I0026604

Practices and Patterns in Research Information Management

Findings from a Global Survey

Rebecca Bryant, Anna Clements, Pablo de Castro, Joanne Cantrell, Annette Dortmund, Jan Fransen, Peggy Gallagher, Michele Mennielli

euroCRIS
Current Research Information Systems

OCLC

Practices and Patterns in Research Information Management: Findings from a Global Survey

Rebecca Bryant
OCLC Research

Anna Clements
University of St Andrews and euroCRIS

Pablo de Castro
University of Strathclyde and euroCRIS

Joanne Cantrell
OCLC

Annette Dortmund
OCLC

Jan Fransen
University of Minnesota, Twin Cities

Peggy Gallagher
OCLC

Michele Mennielli
DuraSpace and euroCRIS

OCLC

euroCRIS
Current Research Information Systems

© 2018 OCLC Online Computer Library Center, Inc.
This work is licensed under a Creative Commons Attribution 4.0 International License.
http://creativecommons.org/licenses/by/4.0/

December 2018

OCLC Research
Dublin, Ohio 43017 USA
www.oclc.org

ISBN: 978-1-55653-073-9
doi: 10.25333/BGFG-D241
OCLC Control Number: 1076929920

ORCID iDs
Rebecca Bryant, https://orcid.org/0000-0002-2753-3881
Anna Clements, https://orcid.org/0000-0003-2895-1310
Pablo de Castro, https://orcid.org/0000-0001-6300-1033
Joanne Cantrell, https://orcid.org/0000-0002-2536-8886
Annette Dortmund, https://orcid.org/0000-0003-1588-9749
Jan Fransen, https://orcid.org/0000-0002-0302-2761
Peggy Gallagher, https://orcid.org/0000-0002-7971-3171
Michele Mennielli, https://orcid.org/0000-0002-4968-906X

Please direct correspondence to:
OCLC Research
oclcresearch@oclc.org

Suggested citation:
Bryant, Rebecca, Anna Clements, Pablo de Castro, Joanne Cantrell, Annette Dortmund, Jan Fransen, Peggy Gallagher, and Michele Mennielli. 2018. *Practices and Patterns in Research Information Management: Findings from a Global Survey*. Dublin, OH: OCLC Research. https://doi.org/10.25333/BGFG-D241.

CONTENTS

FIGURES AND TABLES

FOREWORDS

For some time, I've been observing the increasing role of libraries in supporting research information management (RIM) activities. Already common in countries outside North America, it is now becoming of more interest there also. This is just one part of larger shifts with scholarly communications and the evolving scholarly record, and has interesting connections with broader issues of reputation management in a network environment.

I am pleased to introduce this report which is an important contribution to our knowledge of RIM practices. With responses from over 40 countries, it also gives us an important international perspective.

This report contributes to a growing body of work from OCLC to better understand RIM practices, including their regional differences, as well as the growing interoperability imperative between siloed sources of data—both internal and external. Of particular interest to library readers of this report is the documentation of how university RIM workflows are increasingly intersecting with those in the library, particularly as it relates to the relationship with institutional and data repositories.

We are pleased to have worked collaboratively with euroCRIS on this survey and look forward to repeating the survey in the future, to continue to report to the library community about developments in this emerging component of their service array.

Lorcan Dempsey
Vice President, Membership and Research, Chief Strategist, OCLC

OCLC

Current research information systems (CRISs) were first developed and used in a few European countries at the beginning of the 1990s, and, as the joint euroCRIS-EUNIS CRIS/IR Survey of 2016 showed, have since then been broadly implemented throughout Europe.

Starting as administrative systems for reporting research performance to government, CRISs have evolved in the course of time into multifunctional information systems of use also for research management as well as for the profiling or showcasing of research, both on an individual (researcher) and institutional level. On top of this, more recently, the awareness is growing that, given the richness of interlinked (meta)data on research present in CRISs, these systems could substantially contribute to the FAIRness of research and its products and as such become important building blocks for an open science infrastructure.

The global survey presented in this report builds upon the previously mentioned European survey and shows that both the concept and concrete implementation of CRISs or RIM systems (research information management systems) have started to spread beyond Europe and to take root around the world.

With this growing number of CRISs on a global scale, the issue of interoperability also becomes highly relevant, both between CRISs themselves and with other, complementary systems, such as institutional repositories. After all, to truly leverage the wealth of information available in CRISs it is of importance that they do not remain isolated resources on a local or national level, but become interconnected on an international scale.

Being an organization that on the one hand has a leadership role in promoting the implementation and use of CRIS systems and on the other is the developer and curator of the CERIF (Common European Research Information Format) data model and interoperability standard, euroCRIS warmly applauds and endorses these developments.

This joint survey by euroCRIS and OCLC on research information management systems and practices, the largest ever conducted, not only shows the dynamism of the CRIS/RIM ecosystem, described above, but also is a concrete step toward bringing the global research information community together and promoting the realization of an international research information infrastructure. The comprehensive insights that it provides into many RIM areas makes it worth being regularly followed up in order to identify trends and gradual enhancements on the available RIM infrastructure.

Ed Simons
President, euroCRIS

euroCRIS
Current Research Information Systems

EXECUTIVE SUMMARY

Practices and Patterns in Research Information Management: Findings from a Global Survey represents an effort to better understand how research institutions are applying research information management (RIM) practices. This survey was conducted as part of a strategic partnership between OCLC Research and euroCRIS, and contributes to shared goals to collect quantitative and qualitative data about research information management practices worldwide, to build upon previous research by both organizations, and to provide a baseline of observations for future research.

A web-based survey was administered from 25 October 2017 through 8 February 2018 and yielded 381 survey responses from 44 countries, demonstrating the global nature of research information management activities. This survey employed a convenience sample and the subsequent report is intended to be exploratory and descriptive in nature. A working group comprised of subject matter experts in RIM practices representing both OCLC Research and euroCRIS worked collaboratively to synthesize the data and to write this report.

Research information management practices are complex, and institutions frequently report using several systems to support research information workflows that increasingly demand greater interoperability—with both internal and external systems. Increasingly consolidated commercial and open-source platforms are becoming widely implemented across regions, coexisting with a large number of region-specific solutions as well as locally developed systems. Interoperability is regularly considered a key feature valued or desired in a RIM system, something expected to improve in future systems or configurations, and the use of identifiers, standards, and protocols are perceived as most valuable when they can also facilitate interoperability.

The growing need for improved interoperability between managing open access workflows and the curation of institutional research outputs metadata is giving rise to the increasing functional merging of RIM systems and institutional repositories. This change is being driven in some locales by regional, national, and funder requests to make publicly sponsored research findings openly available—and for institutions to track their progress toward open access goals.

Complex, cross-stakeholder teams are necessary for providing the best possible research support services. Research offices remain leading stakeholders in RIM practices, and the library is also shown to have significant responsibilities, particularly related to support for open access, metadata validation, training, and research data management. Libraries are particularly involved in cases where RIM practices intersect with library responsibility for one or more scholarly communications repositories, reinforcing the increasing overlap of practice and workflows between previously siloed RIM systems and repository systems.

This report frequently emphasizes the analysis of regional differences in order to provide insights on variations in practices and their level of consolidation. By examining research information practices from a global perspective, we are better able to understand the importance and breadth of national research assessment frameworks and open science policies as a key driver strongly shaping priorities of RIM activities in those countries and regions where they exist. In addition, we can also observe an emerging set of additional objectives—such as the desire to improve services for researchers or the need to support institutional reputation and decision-making—that institutions operating in less demanding policy environments see as key incentives for their own RIM strategies.

OCLC Research and euroCRIS plan to repeat this survey in the future, developing longitudinal data and knowledge about evolving RIM practices in order to help inform the global research community.

INTRODUCTION

This report is the culmination of months of collaboration between OCLC Research and euroCRIS. Founded in 2002, euroCRIS is a not-for-profit association that brings together experts on research information in general and current research information systems (CRIS) in particular. Since 1978, OCLC Research has served as one of the world's leading centers devoted exclusively to the challenges facing libraries and archives in a rapidly changing information technology environment, conducting research and piloting technological advances that enhance the value of library services and improve the productivity of librarians and library users.[1]

The two organizations today work together in a strategic partnership to recognize and understand international research information management practices through collaborative research and represent an effort to build closer relationships among librarians, research information administrators and managers, and researchers.[2]

This survey represents the continuation and extension of research by both organizations. In 2016, euroCRIS and EUNIS, the European University Information Systems organization, published the results of a joint survey exploring the interoperability and integration between research information systems (CRIS systems), "managing the institutional research information as a whole including metadata for research papers," and digital repositories, used mainly to "store both metadata and fulltext for publications [...] and dissertations and thesis."[3] OCLC Research has similarly been developing a research agenda on research information management, congruent with its mission to expand knowledge that advances libraries and librarianship, which includes the 2017 *Research Information Management: Defining RIM and the Library's Role*, developed in collaboration with OCLC Research Library Partnership members from three continents.[4]

Based on the definition developed in this position paper, RIM is "the aggregation, curation, and utilization of metadata about research activities" in which "RIM systems collect and store metadata on research activities and outputs such as researchers and their affiliations; publications, datasets, and patents; grants and projects; academic service and honors; media reports; and statements of impact."[5]

RIM development, practices, incentives, and even nomenclature vary broadly by region. In Europe, the concept of RIM appeared as early as 1993, when engagement and oversight was usually the principal domain of the research office. RIM gained new momentum after 2010 as a result of the increasing need for institutions to respond to national-level assessment policies, open access mandates, and the demands of research funders.[6] While Europe has consistently called systems supporting RIM activities Current Research Information Systems (CRIS), now sometimes shortened to Research Information System (RIS) or vernacular equivalents, as demonstrated in the *Science Europe Position Statement on Research Information Systems*,[7] a variety of other terms exist, covering all or just some parts of RIM, especially in regions like North America where research information management practices are newer, and includes terms like Research Networking System (RNS), Research Profiling System (RPS), or Faculty Activity Reporting (FAR).

Research information management practices occur within the larger research ecosystem, intersecting with cultural and technological changes in research practices, a rapidly evolving scholarly record, and increasing efforts to assess research impacts and to make scholarly and scientific outputs broadly and openly available. In our research, we are particularly interested in how RIM practices are being driven (or not) by regional and national mandates, such as research assessment, open access, and open science and data sharing. We are curious to explore how functions, workflows, and stakeholders may be changing and intersecting, and particularly to examine what is anecdotally an increasing role for libraries in research information management.[8]

National research assessment exercises in the UK (Research Excellence Framework, or REF) and Australia (Excellence in Research for Australia, or ERA) require institutions to collect the outputs and measure the impact of sponsored research.[9] In addition to these, there are hundreds of open access mandates, required by scores of funders, research organizations, and national and regional bodies.[10] For example, national funders such as the Research Councils UK (now UKRI), Australian National Health and Medical Research Council (NHMRC), and Australian Research Council (ARC) require publications (and to a lesser degree, research datasets) resulting from funded research projects to be made available in open access form. The European Commission has set a target of having all research outputs freely available by 2020, and European countries are responding with their own individual roadmaps to meet national targets.[11]

Institutions are responding to these external mandates by identifying publications, supporting OA deposit, and using RIM systems to track compliance.[12] Research data is rapidly gaining importance as a first-order research object within the evolving scholarly record, and the retention and long-term curation of research data sets is becoming a part of scholarly practice in many disciplines, both to support replication of published findings as well as to facilitate reuse for new research. National research councils, independent funders, and research universities have all begun to develop services and technologies to support responsible data management.[13]

Survey goals and scope

The overarching goal of this survey is to collect quantitative and qualitative data about research information management practices *worldwide*, and to provide a baseline of observations for future research. While previous efforts to survey regional and national landscapes have taken place, this survey is intended as a first step toward examining the broad global RIM ecosystem.[14] Therefore the survey attempted to be inclusive of all the terms and practices used for and in the context of RIM, seeking input from any institution that is working to collect, curate, and use the metadata about its institutional research footprint.

In our survey, we explored some key areas of interest, each with regional distinctions, where applicable and possible, including:

- the status of RIM system implementations, proprietary and open source solutions in use, and levels of satisfaction with systems
- the incentives for pursuing RIM and important functions of RIM
- the use of RIM systems as a scholarly communications repository
- the roles of institutional stakeholders, including the library
- the growing importance of interoperability and integration with internal and external systems, and the adoption of persistent identifiers, standards, and vocabularies

OCLC Research and euroCRIS plan to repeat this survey in future years, developing longitudinal data and knowledge about evolving practices in order to inform the research community about the changing goals, purposes, and scope of RIM practices. The survey dataset is published and available CC-BY as a companion to this report.[15]

Survey development

A working group of researchers and practitioners from OCLC Research, OCLC Research Library Partnership member institutions, and euroCRIS collaborated throughout 2017 to develop the survey questionnaire. Survey contributors included:

- Rebecca Bryant, OCLC Research
- Pablo de Castro, University of Strathclyde and euroCRIS
- Anna Clements, University of St Andrews and euroCRIS
- Jan Fransen, University of Minnesota, Twin Cities
- Constance Malpas, OCLC Research
- Michele Mennielli, DuraSpace and euroCRIS
- Rachael Samberg, University of California, Berkeley
- Julie Griffin, Virginia Tech

In an effort to report on emerging RIM practices as well as established ones, we designed a survey questionnaire with multiple tracks:

- Live Implementation: For institutions currently live with RIM systems and services publicly visible to campus stakeholders
- In the process of implementing: For institutions where a decision has been made on which RIM system(s) to use, and contracts are signed, but systems and services are not yet operational
- Procurement Process: For institutions in the procurement process, i.e., in the process of evaluating specific systems under consideration
- Exploring: For institutions currently defining system requirements and comparing available options
- Not considering: For institutions not considering RIM systems at this time

As we concluded survey design, we consulted with the market analysis team at OCLC, including Janet Hawk, Peggy Gallagher, and Joanne Cantrell. They improved the survey instrument by enhancing and adding questions, developing survey logic, and providing valuable guidance for compliance with upcoming GDPR requirements.[16] They worked with Marketing Backup, an independent marketing research firm, to develop the internet-based questionnaire.

In September 2017, we engaged 11 beta testers from locales worldwide to provide feedback on the draft survey:

- Carol Feltes, The Rockefeller University
- Bob Gerrity, The University of Queensland
- Paolo Mangiafico, Duke University
- Valerie McCutcheon, University of Glasgow
- Kevin Miller, University of California, Davis
- César Olivares, CONCYTEC
- Jordan Piščanc, University of Trieste
- Birgit Schmidt, Göttingen State and University Library
- Ed Simons, Radboud University and euroCRIS
- Karen Smith-Yoshimura, OCLC Research
- Karla Strieb, The Ohio State University

In the course of our survey development, we also were in contact with CONCYTEC, the Peruvian National Council for Science, Technology and Technological Innovation, which was simultaneously seeking to develop a national assessment of RIM practices and capacities in Peru universities and research institutes.[17] Instead of developing their own survey, they offered to translate this survey into Spanish. As a result, we promoted both English and Spanish language versions of the survey instrument.[18]

Marketing Backup administered the finalized survey from 25 October 2017 through 8 February 2018.

Getting the survey in front of the right people was probably the biggest challenge of this project. RIM managers and leaders might be situated in research offices, libraries, or elsewhere in their organizations. This makes it impossible to seek participation from a predefined list of RIM practitioners, or through a single professional advocacy organization; the diversity of practices and practitioners is a huge barrier to identifying potential participants upfront. This is an additional aspect in which this project will provide foundational information and lessons learned for future research efforts.

To promote the survey broadly, OCLC Research, euroCRIS, and members of the survey working group used blog posts, newsletter items, distribution lists, presentations, and announcements through OCLC and euroCRIS channels, as well as engaged partner networks worldwide.

For instance, we invited known vendors and open source providers of RIM products to share the survey with user group communities and clients. Vendors contacted included Elsevier, Digital Science, Digital Measures, Interfolio, Clarivate Analytics, Omega-PSIR, 4Science, and Sigma. We also promoted the survey to the Duraspace community and invited members of the Profiles RNS listserv to participate.

We leveraged our own networks to raise awareness, contacting individuals at consortial, library, and research organizations worldwide, providing them with information and messaging to help us promote survey participation. For instance, members of the OCLC Research Library Partnership in Australia helped to promote the survey through their engagement with regional organizations, including posting to listservs and newsletters hosted by:

- Australian Library and Information Association (ALIA)
- Australian National Data Service (ANDS)
- Australasian Research Management Society (ARMS)
- Council of Australasian University Directors of Information Technology (CAUDIT)
- Council of Australian University Librarians (CAUL)
- Group of Eight (Go8)
- Universities Australia (UA)

In Europe, we contacted a number of organizations, including:

- Association of Research Managers and Administrators (ARMA, UK)
- Cineca, Italy
- Confederation of Open Access Repositories (COAR)
- Deutsche Initiative für Netzwerkinformation e. V. (DINI FIS)
- European Association of Research Managers and Administrators (EARMA)
- European University Information Systems (EUNIS)
- InetBib (Internet in Bibliotheken)
- Jisc
- Ligue des Bibliothèques Européennes de Recherche (Association of European Research Libraries, LIBER)
- Research Libraries UK

And in the Americas, we sought the assistance of:

- Association of American Universities Data Exchange (AAUDE)
- Association of College & Research Libraries (ACRL)
- Association for Information Science & Technology (ASIS&T)
- Association of Institutional Research (AIR)
- Big Ten Academic Alliance (BTAA)
- Canadian Association of Research Libraries (CARL)
- Coalition for Networked Information (CNI)
- National Organization of Research Development Professionals (NORDP)
- The Peruvian National Council for Science, Technology and Technological Innovation (CONCYTEC)
- Lista Latinoamericana sobre Acceso Abierto y Repositorios (LLAAR)

- U15, group of Canadian research universities (Canadian top 15 research universities)

Finally, we sought the support of international standards and identifiers organizations:

- Consortia Advancing Standards in Research Administration Information (CASRAI)
- ORCID

CONCYTEC in Peru and Cineca in Italy were particularly enthusiastic in their promotion of the survey within their countries, and the results show, with 39 and 28 responding institutions, respectively. In Australia, ARMS particularly encouraged members to participate, and likely drove our good response from Australian institutions.

Survey analysis and limitations

This survey employed a convenience sample and was intended to be exploratory and descriptive. As these samples are not random nor directly comparable, this analysis should be treated as suggestive rather than conclusive and provides a foundation for future research. Our working group comprised of subject matter experts in RIM practices worked collaboratively to synthesize the data and to write this report. We have done no coding or counting of verbatim comments. We consulted with others in OCLC marketing analysis when we had questions about the sample.

The OCLC Research-euroCRIS Survey of Research Information Management Practices received 381 survey responses from 44 countries, which demonstrates the global nature of research information management activities.

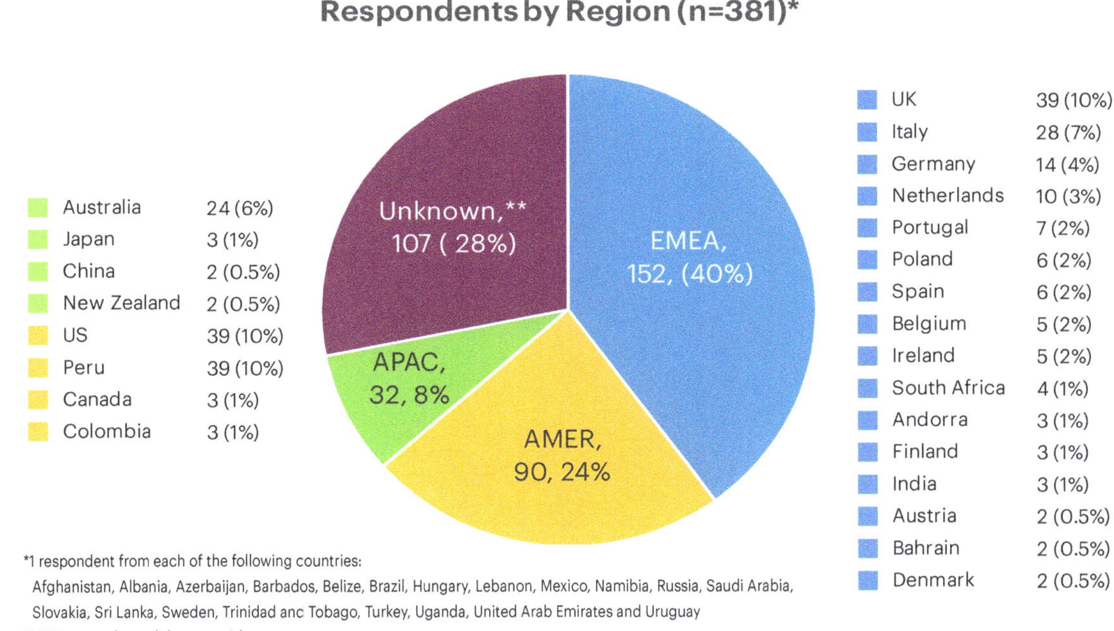
Respondents by Region (n=381)*
Australia 24 (6%)
Japan 3 (1%)
China 2 (0.5%)
New Zealand 2 (0.5%)
US 39 (10%)
Peru 39 (10%)
Canada 3 (1%)
Colombia 3 (1%)
Unknown,** 107 (28%)
EMEA, 152, (40%)
APAC, 32, 8%
AMER, 90, 24%
UK 39 (10%)
Italy 28 (7%)
Germany 14 (4%)
Netherlands 10 (3%)
Portugal 7 (2%)
Poland 6 (2%)
Spain 6 (2%)
Belgium 5 (2%)
Ireland 5 (2%)
South Africa 4 (1%)
Andorra 3 (1%)
Finland 3 (1%)
India 3 (1%)
Austria 2 (0.5%)
Bahrain 2 (0.5%)
Denmark 2 (0.5%)
*1 respondent from each of the following countries:
Afghanistan, Albania, Azerbaijan, Barbados, Belize, Brazil, Hungary, Lebanon, Mexico, Namibia, Russia, Saudi Arabia, Slovakia, Sri Lanka, Sweden, Trinidad anc Tobago, Turkey, Uganda, United Arab Emirates and Uruguay
** 107 respondents did not provide a country

FIGURE 1. Total number of survey respondents, by broad region. EMEA = Europe, Middle East, Africa; AMER = Americas; APAC = Asia-Pacific.

While analyzing the data, we reviewed responses in aggregate but also were looking for regional patterns by reviewing responses for individual countries and selected regions. Unfortunately, 65 of the 222 respondents with a live RIM system and 24 respondents implementing one did not indicate their country, significantly reducing useful sample sizes for regional analysis. However, even though many of the per country samples are small, they are sometimes quite representative. For instance, nine of 12 research universities in the Netherlands responded to this questionnaire; samples in the UK, Australia, and Italy are also fairly representative. We particularly recognize the weakness of the US sample in this study but have chosen to include it where applicable, as we believe it can still suggest regional differences of interest. This is sometimes true for other countries as well.

Survey respondents represented a diversity of institutional practice, where no single unit or area of responsibility dominated. We heard from practitioners in libraries and research administration offices; for each of those areas, nearly half of the respondents indicated having responsibility in either area, with some overlap, as 14% (n=39) of respondents indicated having responsibilities in both research administration and the library.

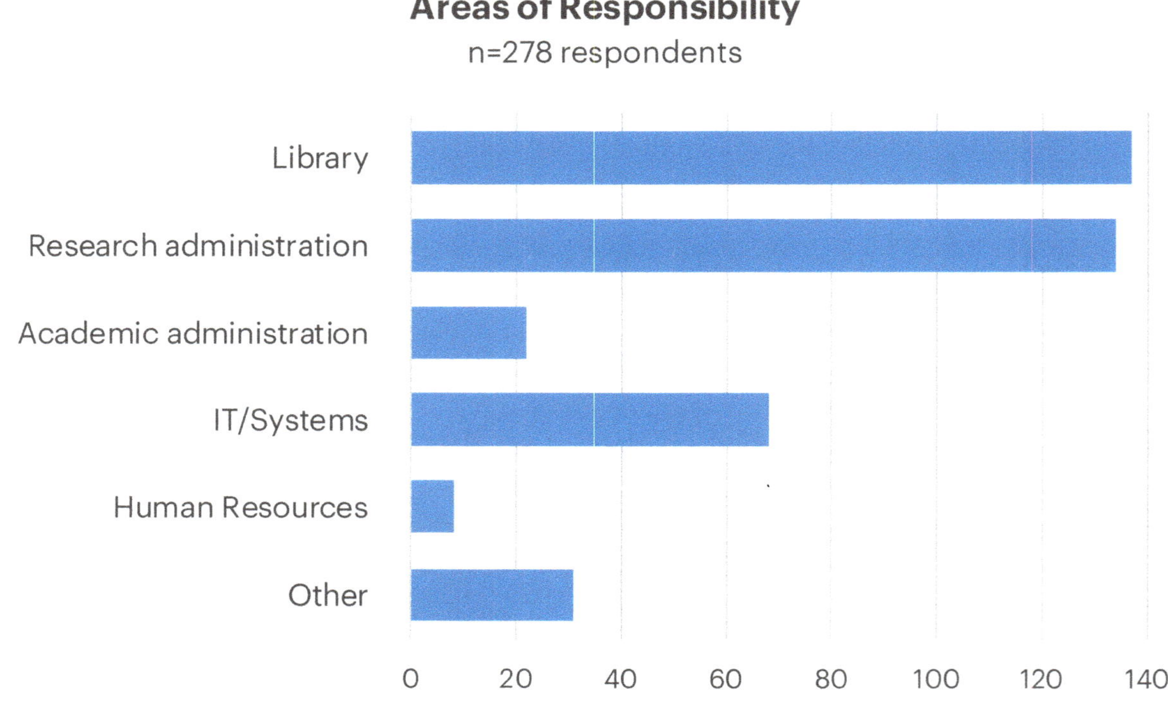
Areas of Responsibility
n=278 respondents
Library
Research administration
Academic administration
IT/Systems
Human Resources
Other
0
20
40
60
80
100
120
140

FIGURE 2. Areas of responsibility of survey respondents, where respondents could select more than one option.

There are inherent difficulties in evaluating RIM practices internationally. As detailed above, RIM practices, uses, drivers, maturity, scope, and nomenclature vary broadly by region, making the effort to collect broad, international findings much more complicated and challenging than pursuing a smaller, more homogenous regional or national study. In particular, the authors want to acknowledge the following limitations:

1. The survey results have been significantly impacted by the specific efforts to disseminate information about the survey and recruit participation. As described above, seeking survey participation from RIM practitioners directly, or through a single professional organization, was not possible. Instead, the survey development team relied heavily upon existing networks

and communication channels to promote the survey, potentially leading to overrepresentation in some areas and underrepresentation in others. This limitation was understood from the very beginning of our project.

Samples are too small to be significant for compelling regional analysis. For the United States and Canada, a total of only 42 institutions responded to the survey, 22 of which were from institutions with live RIM systems. There are fewer responses still from Asia, Africa, and parts of South America, except for Peru: 39 of the 47 South/Central American and Caribbean responses were from Peru.[19] Responses from some countries with significant RIM activity such as Norway or France are missing. This is likely related to survey dissemination or the emphasis on institutional RIM practices rather than national-level efforts, as practiced in Norway. In contrast, we also had enthusiastic participation from countries like Italy and Peru, which both worked nationally to promote survey participation among their constituents.

Understanding that RIM is still undergoing adoption in many parts of the world, we offered survey respondents the opportunity to engage, regardless of their implementation status. This yielded a healthy sample for live implementations (n=222) but much smaller samples for institutions in the state of implementing (n=51), procuring (n=13), exploring (n=46), and not considering (n=49). We have focused the majority of this report on responses from institutions with live RIM implementations, sometimes supplementing with information from institutions at other stages of implementation, when it seems relevant.

Some questions, even among institutions with live RIM implementations, yielded few responses. Due to these small samples, we have not discussed these results in the report. Specific questions with few responses include questions about medical centers/hospitals and disciplinary subject areas included in the RIM system. While we received an adequate response to questions about when implementation and launch occurred, the survey design seemed to have confused respondents, and we decided not to report findings. Questions about the number of researcher and scholar records in RIM systems also seemed to cause confusion; some respondents were uncertain whether this was intended to include all researchers and scholars including past employees, or just those with a current affiliation.

2. A related problem is the lack of standard nomenclature about research information management practices, which likely prevented many target respondents from recognizing that this survey was relevant to them. For example, European respondents are most familiar with the term "CRIS," which is largely unused in North America, where an alphabet soup of terms are proliferating as the ecosystem matures. We sought responses from any institution collecting metadata about its research footprint, for any use, including research networking, and note an underrepresentation of institutions using open source VIVO and Profiles RNS research networking products.[20]
3. Another interrelated problem was getting the survey in front of the right person *within* an institution, as RIM managers and leaders might be situated in research offices, libraries, IT, or elsewhere in their organizations. The workflows around RIM as a whole and around specific aspects of it, such as open science policy implementation, have a significant level of overlap, but the institutional units dealing with each of them are frequently unaware of the developments in each others' camps. And while we asked respondents to answer questions on behalf of their entire institution, we recognize that institutional silos and complexity of practice may make this difficult to achieve.[21]

4. Our ability to interpret regional and national findings are further compromised by the fact that nearly 30% of respondents did not indicate their country, as we did not make this a required field. We took a cautious approach to collecting identifying information because of pending GDPR rules; we will reassess this practice in future surveys.
5. In an effort to better understand the development of RIM practices where adoption is still taking place, we invited institutions to participate if they were exploring or implementing RIM capacity. Unfortunately, this effort resulted in greater complexity, some confusion among survey respondents, and small samples.
6. Survey fatigue is also a probable factor and limitation in our results, particularly as this survey follows only two years after the euroCRIS/EUNIS survey on CRIS/IR practices from 2015.

Despite these acknowledged limitations, we believe this survey provides a much-needed beginning for study of global RIM practices and can provide a basis for future international, regional, and national research. As mentioned above, euroCRIS and OCLC Research intend to repeat this survey in the future, which offers an opportunity to address these limitations and develop a more robust, longitudinal understanding of evolving research information management practices, stakeholders, and incentives.

Findings

Status of RIM system implementations overall

Respondents were presented with five different statuses of RIM system implementation and were asked to indicate which status best applied to their institution. Over half (58%) of the respondents currently have a live system and another 13% are in the process of implementing RIM capacity. Four percent (4%) are in the procurement process, 12% are exploring, and 13% are not currently considering implementing a RIM system.

The majority of this research report will focus on the responses of institutions with RIM system(s) in production (also called live), with additional analysis, when applicable, from survey respondents describing their implementation, procurement, and exploration activities.

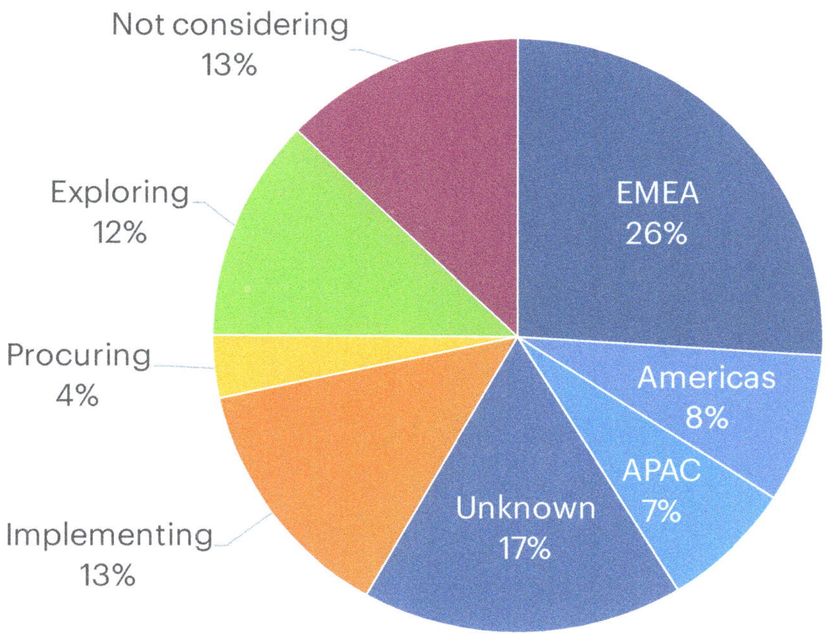
Respondents by RIM Status (n=381)
Note: 29 respondents did not provide their RIM system
Not considering
13%
Exploring
12%
Procuring
4%
Implementing
13%
EMEA
26%
Americas
8%
APAC
7%
Unknown
17%

FIGURE 3. Implementation status of survey respondents. EMEA is Europe, Middle East, Africa; and APAC is Asia-Pacific.

RIM products and systems

RIM PRODUCTS IN USE

We asked respondents with a live RIM system to indicate which product or products they use. Of the 222 respondents with a live RIM system, 30 did not indicate the products supporting their RIM system. One hundred forty-eight specified only one product, and the remaining 44 (23%) specified two or more products used in combination; in the majority of these cases a system developed in-house is combined with one of the other solutions listed. One respondent commented,

> "At [institution name] our Research Information Management activities are supported across a few systems, as opposed to a single integrated RIM, and the primary system is our project management system as that drives our business." **(Australia)**

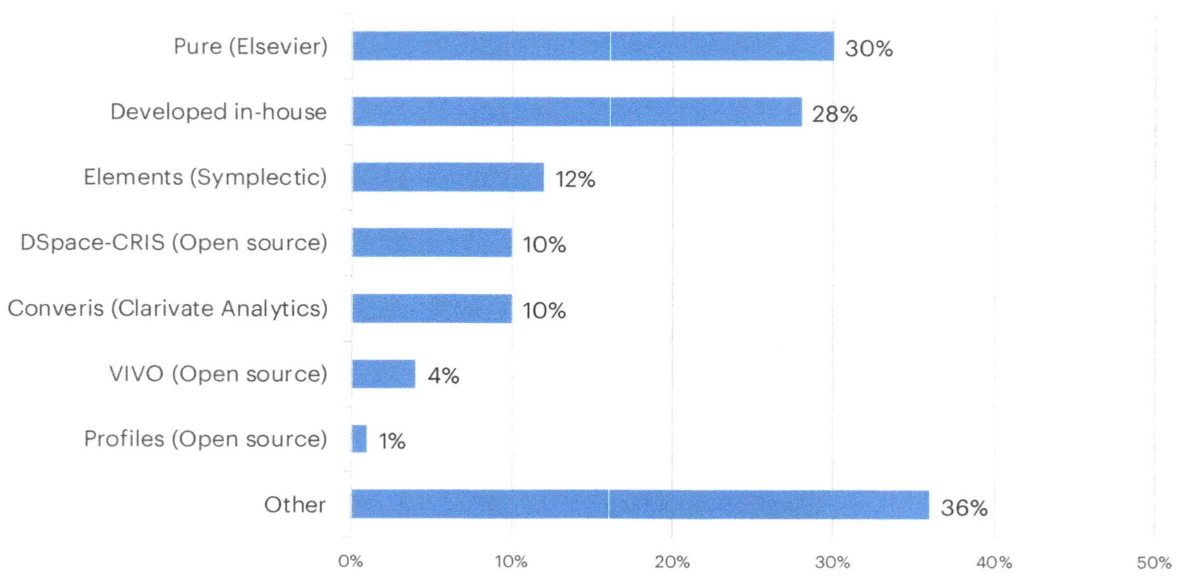
RIM Systems in Use by Survey Respondents (n=193)
Note: 29 respondents did not provide their RIM system
Pure (Elsevier)
30%
Developed in-house
28%
Elements (Symplectic)
12%
DSpace-CRIS (Open source)
10%
Converis (Clarivate Analytics)
10%
VIVO (Open source)
4%
Profiles (Open source)
1%
Other
36%
0%
10%
20%
30%
40%
50%

FIGURE 4. RIM systems in use by institutions with live RIM implementations.

Another described the migration of one system while maintaining the other in the RIM ecosystem.

> "The University will be migrating to a new grants management system (from Info Ed). Pure will remain to manage other RIM aspects." **(Australia)**

Over a third (36%) indicated they use an "other" RIM system, often one of particular regional importance, with the most-mentioned systems being Cineca's IRIS (n=25), Research Master (n=5), InfoEd, and OMEGA-PSIR (n=4, each).

Among survey respondents currently implementing a RIM solution, when asked "What RIM system(s) is your institution currently implementing?" half of the respondents reported that they are currently implementing a system developed in-house. Roughly half of those, among them a relatively large group of institutions from Peru, indicated they are implementing an in-house system to work in conjunction with a DSpace or DSpace-CRIS implementation.

This is congruent with our observations in the section System migration, below, which also revealed how systems developed in-house continue to play an important role, and that institutions often use several systems in conjunction, seeking to integrate or complement one with the other.

Regional distribution of these products

While we found the use of Pure and in-house systems worldwide, the use of several products is highly regionalized.

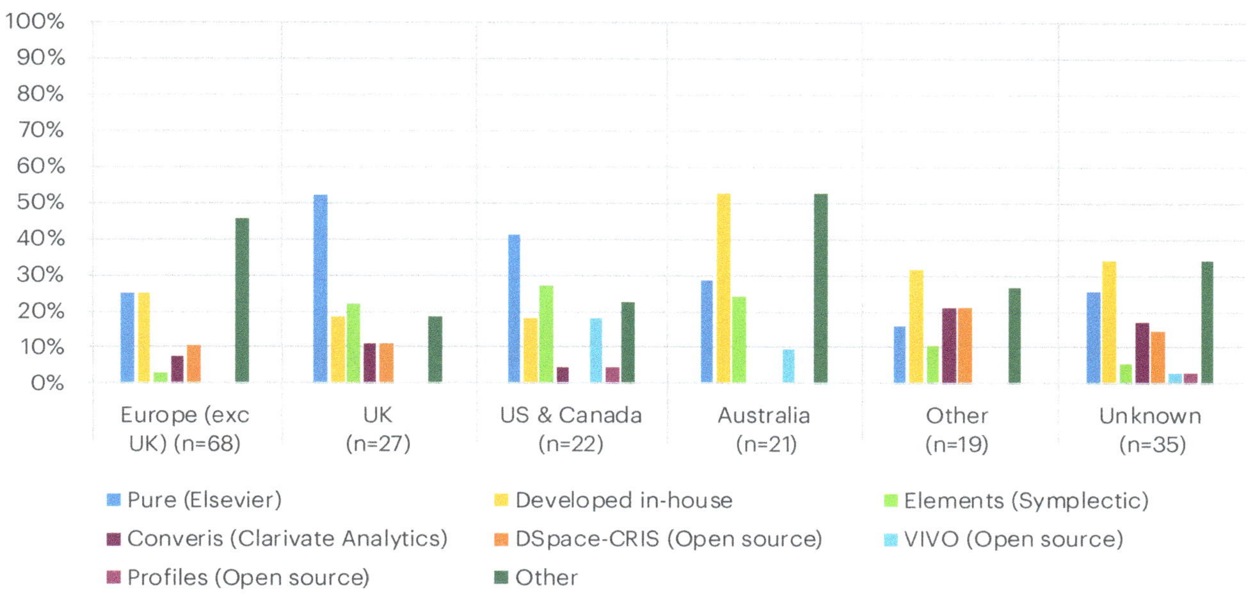
Live RIM Systems in Use by Geography
100%
90%
80%
70%
60%
50%
40%
30%
20%
10%
0%
Europe (exc UK) (n=68)
UK (n=27)
US & Canada (n=22)
Australia (n=21)
Other (n=19)
Unknown (n=35)
Pure (Elsevier)
Developed in-house
Elements (Symplectic)
Converis (Clarivate Analytics)
DSpace-CRIS (Open source)
VIVO (Open source)
Profiles (Open source)
Other

FIGURE 5. Live RIM systems in use, by selected regions.

We analyzed regional-based distribution of the above mentioned RIM systems. It is worth noticing that DSpace-CRIS and Converis are more popular in Europe in comparison to other parts of the world, most likely because of their European origin.[22] The survey responses also demonstrate that distribution of the Symplectic Elements product is aligned almost exclusively with primarily English-speaking locales: the US, Canada, UK, and Australia. The open source VIVO platform, a solution known as a discovery tool for scientists, is similarly represented primarily in the US and Australia. Elsevier's Pure is comparatively popular across all regions. Europe and Australia both make much use of "other" systems. Among those European institutions that mentioned "others" as their institutional RIM system, nearly every institution in Italy (22 out of 23) indicated they use IRIS-CINECA—a RIM system based on open source technologies and focused on the Italian market.[23] Four institutions in Australia report using research administration solutions from InfoEd[24] always in conjunction with other systems (Elements, Pure, or a system developed in-house) to cover additional areas of RIM. Four Australian institutions use solutions from ResearchMaster, an Australian-based research management system provider,[25] either standalone (2) or in combination with Symplectic Elements (2).

These findings demonstrate the widespread, international usage of some systems as well as the more regional distribution of others.

HOSTING LOCATION OF CURRENT RIM SYSTEM

Respondents were asked if their current RIM system is hosted externally or on campus.

Not surprisingly, the majority of RIM systems developed in-house are hosted on campus (89%) as well as 20 of 23 Elements instances. All instances of the OMEGA-PSIR[26] and nearly all (six of seven) of the VIVO implementations are hosted locally.

Pure instances vary, with 13 of 14 UK instances hosted locally, but all seven US instances hosted externally, which may be the result of older UK Pure implementations that pre-dated a cloud-hosted option. Overall, 58% of Pure instances are hosted on-campus. The majority of respondents using IRIS systems completing the survey say they are now hosted externally (92%).

For the remainder of systems, hosting is split between those hosted on campus and those hosted externally.

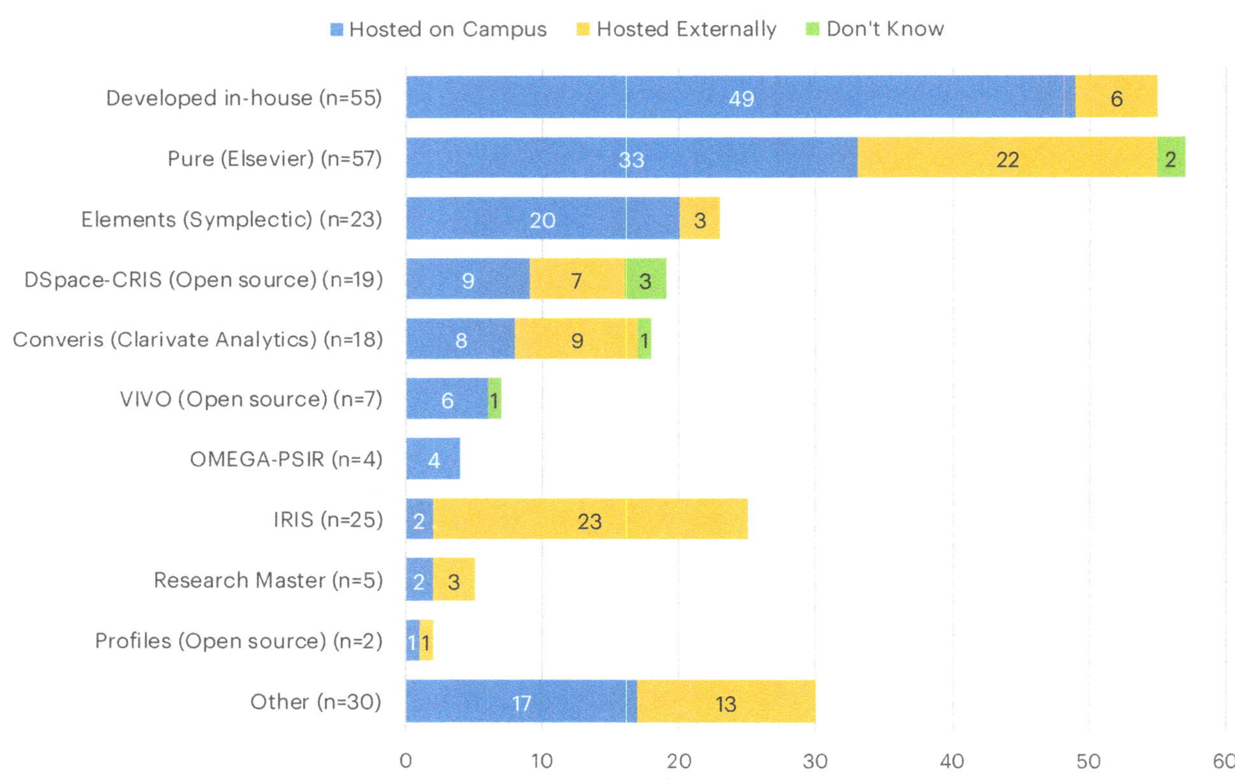

Hosting Location of Current Live RIM System
Hosted on Campus
Hosted Externally
Don't Know
Developed in-house (n=55)
49
6
Pure (Elsevier) (n=57)
33
22
2
Elements (Symplectic) (n=23)
20
3
DSpace-CRIS (Open source) (n=19)
9
7
3
Converis (Clarivate Analytics) (n=18)
8
9
1
VIVO (Open source) (n=7)
6
1
OMEGA-PSIR (n=4)
4
IRIS (n=25)
2
23
Research Master (n=5)
2
3
Profiles (Open source) (n=2)
1
1
Other (n=30)
17
13
0
10
20
30
40
50
60

FIGURE 6. Hosting location of current live RIM system, per system used.

SATISFACTION AND RECOMMENDATION OF CURRENT RIM SYSTEM

Respondents were asked to indicate their level of satisfaction with their current RIM system, with options ranging from very satisfied to not at all satisfied.

Among those systems with at least 16 respondents, Elements from Symplectic has the highest satisfaction rate at 91%.

- Elements: 20 of 22 (91%) are satisfied
- Developed in-house: 45 of 53 (85%)
- Pure: 48 of 57 (84%)
- DSpace-CRIS: 16 of 19 (84%)
- IRIS: 18 of 23 (78%)
- Converis: 11 of 18 (61%)

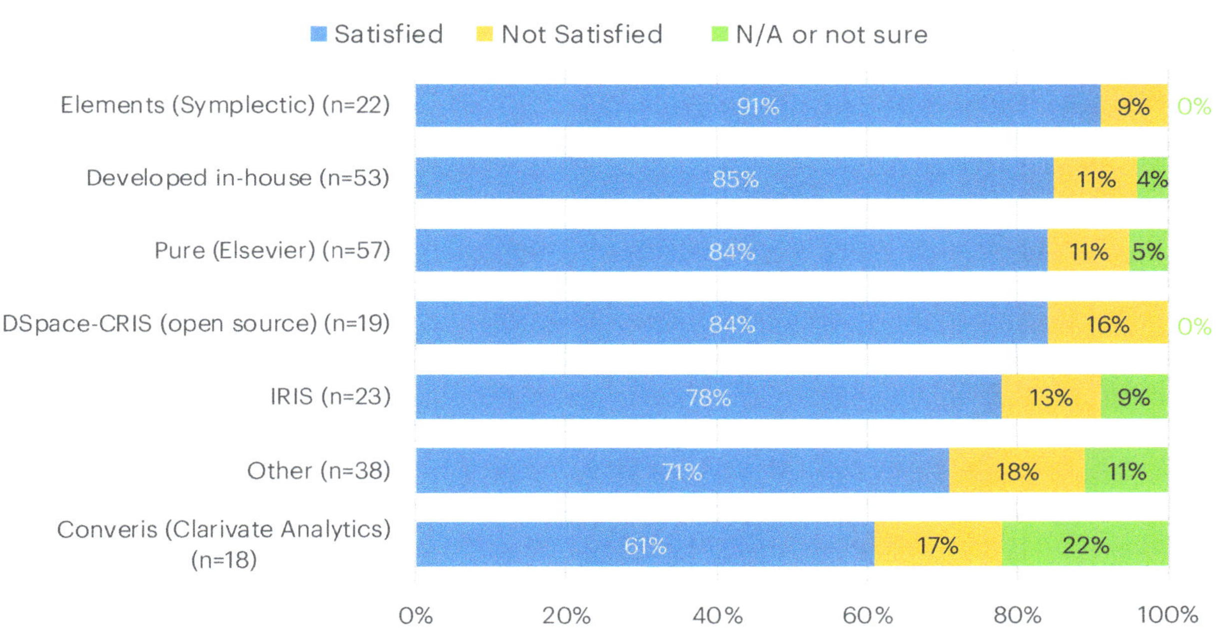

Satisfaction with Current RIM System
Satisfied
Not Satisfied
N/A or not sure
Elements (Symplectic) (n=22)
91%
9%
0%
Developed in-house (n=53)
85%
11%
4%
Pure (Elsevier) (n=57)
84%
11%
5%
DSpace-CRIS (open source) (n=19)
84%
16%
0%
IRIS (n=23)
78%
13%
9%
Other (n=38)
71%
18%
11%
Converis (Clarivate Analytics) (n=18)
61%
17%
22%
0%
20%
40%
60%
80%
100%

FIGURE 7. Satisfaction levels, per live RIM system used.

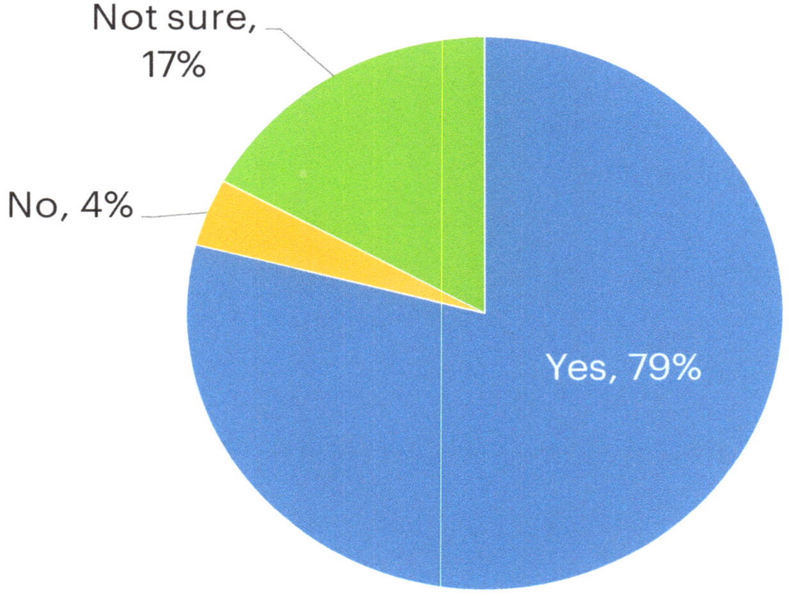
Would You Recommend to Others the RIM System You are Currently Using? (N=155)
Not sure, 17%
No, 4%
Yes, 79%

FIGURE 8. Institutions recommending their current live RIM system to others (Y/N/Not sure).

When asked if they would recommend their RIM solution to other institutions, more than three-fourths (79%) would recommend, few would not (4%), and 17% were not sure.

Open-ended comments illustrate what drives satisfaction and dissatisfaction for commercial and open source systems:[27]

> "System can be adapted to individual & changing needs. Room for improvement at provider: internal & external communication, reaction on specific needs of a national user group." **(Germany)**

> "We are dealing with mature products which are actively maintained/updated and have good engagement with the user community." **(UK)**

> "We have collaborated very successfully with the company over the years to help with the development of new functionality at technical and customer levels. They are very responsive to our institutional requirements and it is a data source for many other systems." **(New Zealand)**

> "While there are occasional shortcomings in terms of its adaptation to specific workflows—mainly resulting from the very large customer base with specific needs for the CRIS platform—our current level of user satisfaction is high. Open Access should however be highlighted as an area where possible improvements could definitely be pointed out." **(UK)**

> "The automatic publication harvesting has been a hit with our science (and some social-science) faculty. It could do a better job of supporting Humanities publications, and needs work in the creative works arena." **(US)**
>
> "Ability to import from ORCID is not corrently [sic] available. Ability to update metadata recrods [sic] once created is not acurrently [sic] available. This is a big problem and means that the metadata in our RIM is reducing in quality." **(Country unknown)**
>
> "Would like more integrations with other systems such as Figshare." **(UK)**

For systems developed in-house, these verbatim comments illustrate typical scenarios:

> "The flexibility of an in-house solution allows us to easily adapt to constant change in the needs of the researchers, research centres and reporting workflows." **(Portugal)**
>
> "Pure promised a lot as a stand-alone program that it has not delivered. Even though we have integrated it with our in-house RIM in order to track hires, promotions, terminations, etc. as well as projects/grants, we find that it still takes more personal follow-up to make things work correctly than is desired." **(US)**
>
> "The in-house developed solution allows us to have full control and flexibility to answer the requirements imposed by the stakeholders, whereas DSpace, although working as expected, does introduce some limitations that are not easy to manage." **(Portugal)**
>
> "The in-house system is flexible in meeting the changing needs of publication management and gives a degree of control over those changes. Less satisfied with its lack of interoperability with other systems—as it is a bespoke system, it lacks the benefit of having a community of developers." **(Australia)**

SYSTEM MIGRATION

Migration from a previous RIM system

Respondents with live RIM systems were asked if they had migrated from a previous RIM, and, if so, which system and for what reasons. Just over half (55%) of respondents reported migrating from a previous system, which in the majority of cases was from a system developed in-house or a wide range of other, often region-specific, systems (such as U-GOV Ricerca or Metis),[28] not one of the established open source or commercial systems offered as response options in the survey. The other 45% indicated having had no prior RIM system.

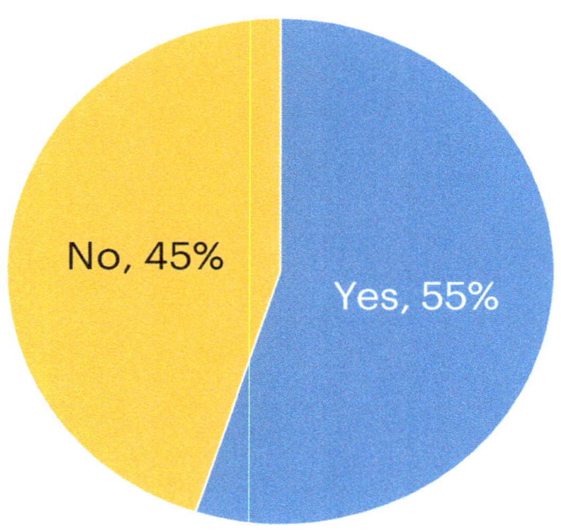
Did You Migrate from a Previous RIM System? (n=189)
No, 45%
Yes, 55%

FIGURE 9. Institutions reporting having migrated from previous live RIM system.

The open-ended comments to this question inform us about the reasons for system migration, including the lack of functionality or the unsustainability of previous systems; end of life of the previous product; or a perceived need for new technology, functionality, or integration. Survey respondents said:

> "Aging infrastructure needed to be replaced. As it was in-house, the person that developed it had left the institution leaving no expertise for the system." **(Australia)**

> "The in-house system was no longer being supported by our IT services team." **(Canada)**

> "Lack of functionality. End of life for Digitool. Need to consolidate systems." **(Australia)**

> "Previous system unsustainable. Terrible usability." **(Colombia, translated from Spanish)**

> "A more integrated workflow and to also make it more attractive to the Researcher and easier to use." **(Australia)**

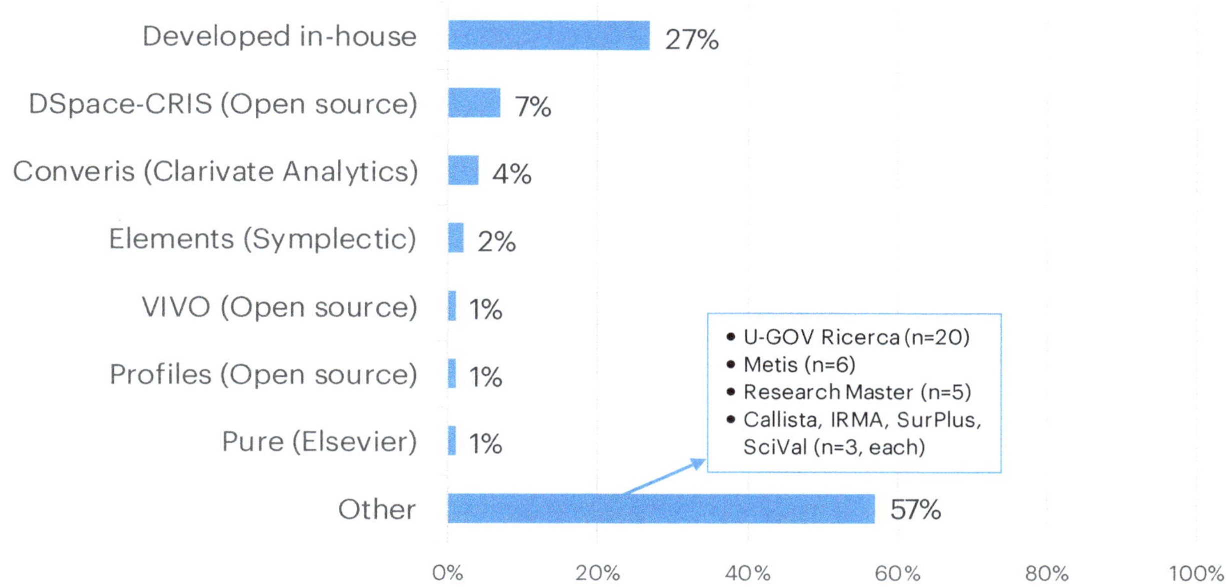
Previous RIM System (n=104)
Developed in-house
DSpace-CRIS (Open source)
Converis (Clarivate Analytics)
Elements (Symplectic)
VIVO (Open source)
Profiles (Open source)
Pure (Elsevier)
Other
27%
7%
4%
2%
1%
1%
1%
57%
• U-GOV Ricerca (n=20)
• Metis (n=6)
• Research Master (n=5)
• Callista, IRMA, SurPlus, SciVal (n=3, each)
0%
20%
40%
60%
80%
100%

FIGURE 10. Previous RIM systems of institutions with a live RIM system that migrated from a previous RIM system.

In comparison, institutions in the process of currently implementing a RIM system indicated *not* migrating from a previous system in two-thirds of the cases (n=42); this is partly due to a comparatively large group of institutions from Peru indicating no prior RIM experience.

RIM systems are still a relatively young product category

The fact that many institutions with a live RIM today either have a RIM system for the first time or have moved to their current system from a locally developed or regional system is indicative that RIM systems are still a relatively young product category. As noted above, the level of market penetration by well-established, feature-rich, mature systems, commercial or otherwise, is still low in some regions, although satisfaction with the products once implemented is often high.

Anticipated future system migration

Respondents with live RIM systems were asked if they anticipate their institution will migrate from their current RIM in the foreseeable future. Under a fifth of institutions (17%) do anticipate migrating from their current RIM, which is not surprising given satisfaction levels with current systems.

Overall, the open-ended responses to this question by those anticipating future system migration indicate a general openness to future migrations as well as dissatisfaction with current systems; it also reveals the multitude of systems sometimes associated with RIM and the need for integration and interoperability.

"Our University Policy dictates: 1.) A 'Buy not Build' policy. B.) All applications need to be cloud hosted. C.) To source key market systems which tend to generally have significantly improved capabilities. D.) Current system is based on old technology and uses dysfunctional features." **(Australia)**

"I expect that within the next few years there will be better software options that enable integrations etc." **(Canada)**

"The University will be migrating to a new grants management system (from Info Ed). Pure will remain to manage other RIM aspects." **(Australia)**

"We're keeping VIVO, but we are likely starting over as we have a new system in place to export all information into VIVO. Additionally, our IT department will take it over and start it over." **(US)**

SUMMARY: SYSTEM SUPPORT FOR RIM

"They are not very well developed compared to integrated library systems. They are also being asked to do things that they were not designed for. Their role and use really needs to be considered to see what direction they should be going." **(Australia)**

Systems supporting RIM are still a young product category, and many institutions currently implementing or live with a RIM system indicate no prior RIM system experience.

Mature, feature-rich products exist, both as commercial and open source solutions, which usually indicates a maturing market. On the other hand, **systems developed in-house still play an important role**, as do systems of national or regional relevance or provenance. While the survey is not sufficiently representative for all regions, the conclusion that **product preferences are highly regionalized** can be safely drawn. It is worth noting that **institutions often use several systems in concert**, which indicates that, although satisfaction with the individual products is often very high, **no individual product alone can meet all their needs**. The need to use multiple products to address different parts of the research information workflow is likely due to the complex incentives and uses driving RIM practice. The need to interoperate with a growing number of areas, constituents, and systems will be further explored in the next section of this report.

RIM incentives and uses

Based on former experiences and current daily use of RIM systems, the working group was aware of the main reasons why institutions choose to implement a RIM strategy. However, some of this awareness was based on the work within a highly advanced environment where a complex network of research assessment and open science policies are in place, and there was some interest in what the main incentives and uses might be under different circumstances. Also, we posited that perceptions of RIM might be different among those working with established RIM infrastructure and those in nascent environments.

To capture the multiple facets of this complex web of incentives and functions, we asked respondents three separate questions related to their perceptions of research information management and the systems to support it:

- Why did your institution pursue RIM activities? **(Reasons for pursuing RIM activities)**
- Which RIM functions are important to your institution? **(RIM functions)**
- How important are specific incentives for scholars and researchers to use the RIM system(s) at your institution? **(Researcher incentives for using RIM systems)**

First, we examine these separately, then analyze relevant RIM uses more deeply in context.

REASONS FOR PURSUING RIM ACTIVITIES

We examined responses to the survey questions by looking first at what seemed to be the most important drivers for all institutions that have a live RIM system. As we anticipated, two main incentives—reporting on the institutional research activity and ensuring institutional compliance with open science policies—came out clearly on top.

Importance of Reasons for Pursuing RIM Activities (n=222)

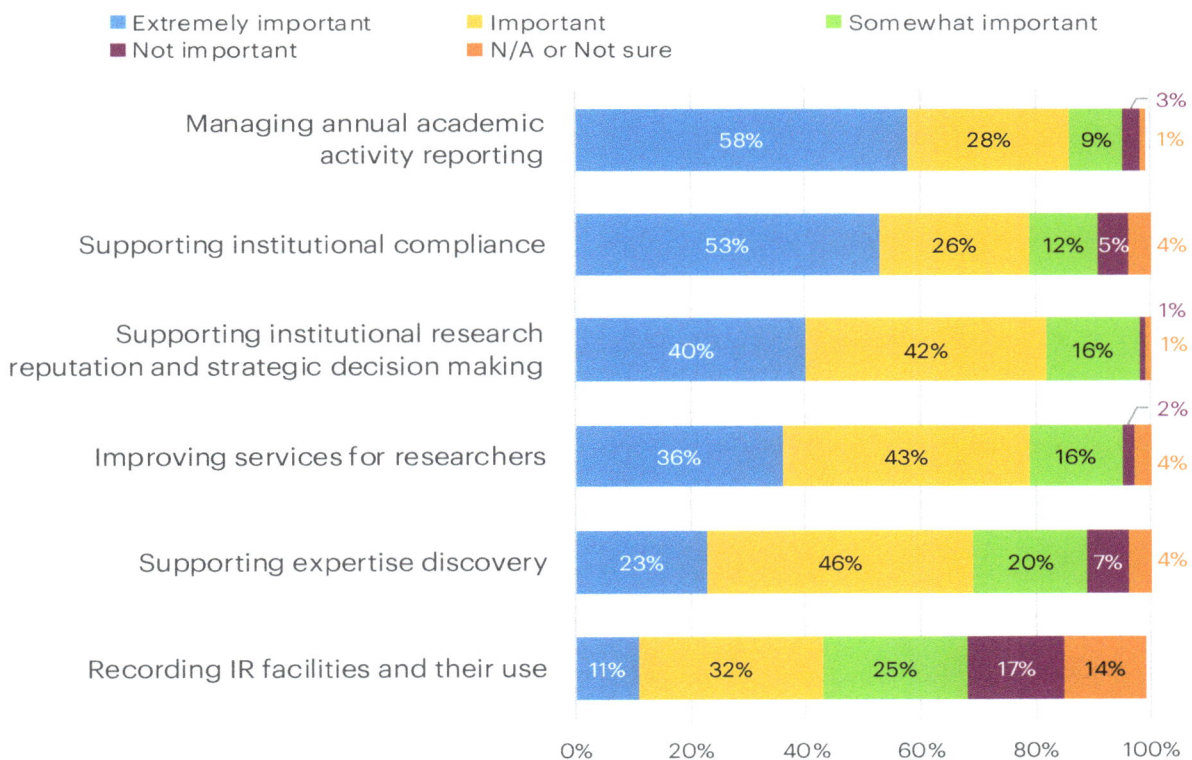

	Extremely important	Important	Somewhat important	Not important	N/A or Not sure
Managing annual academic activity reporting	58%	28%	9%	3%	1%
Supporting institutional compliance	53%	26%	12%	5%	4%
Supporting institutional research reputation and strategic decision making	40%	42%	16%	1%	1%
Improving services for researchers	36%	43%	16%	2%	4%
Supporting expertise discovery	23%	46%	20%	7%	4%
Recording IR facilities and their use	11%	32%	25%	17%	14%

0% 20% 40% 60% 80% 100%

FIGURE 11. Importance of reasons for pursuing RIM activities for institutions with a live RIM system (n=222).

When comparing this to institutions currently implementing RIM systems, we noticed that the priority of reasons and levels of importance for pursuing RIM capacity differed slightly.

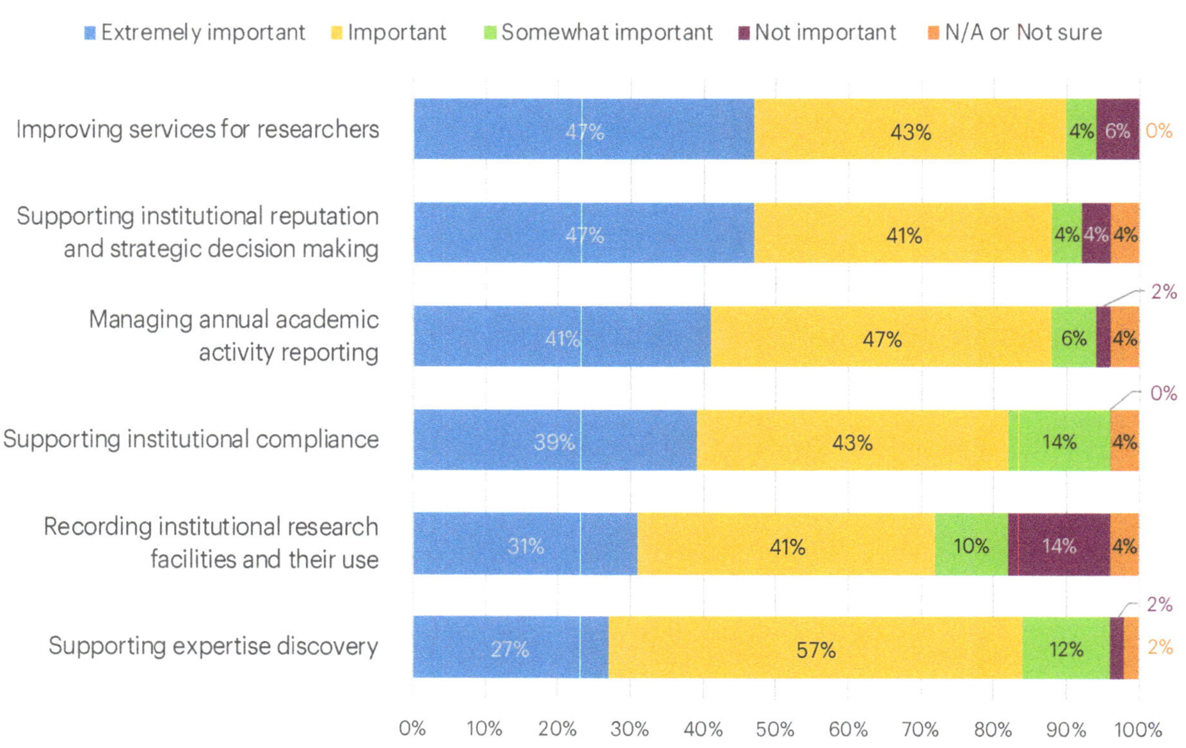
Activities for Institutions Implementing RIM Systems (n=51)
Extremely important
Important
Somewhat important
Not important
N/A or Not sure
Improving services for researchers
47%
43%
4%
6%
0%
Supporting institutional reputation and strategic decision making
47%
41%
4%
4%
4%
Managing annual academic activity reporting
41%
47%
6%
2%
4%
Supporting institutional compliance
39%
43%
14%
0%
4%
Recording institutional research facilities and their use
31%
41%
10%
14%
4%
Supporting expertise discovery
27%
57%
12%
2%
2%
0%
10%
20%
30%
40%
50%
60%
70%
80%
90%
100%

FIGURE 12. Importance of reasons for pursuing RIM activities for institutions implementing RIM systems (n=51).

Given survey limitations, these results should not be overinterpreted, but they could suggest a change, or at least broadening of purpose, as more institutions implement RIM systems under different policy scenarios. The results hint at a trend that more institutions in countries not subject to national reporting mandates are starting to implement RIM systems. This is an effect the working group was keen to identify: the outcome would seem to suggest that where there may be weaker requirements with regard to research assessment or mandatory open access and research data management policies, incentives like improving services for researchers and supporting the institutional reputation and decision-making come to the fore instead. However, almost half of the respondents at institutions implementing RIM did not specify their country (24 of 51), so no meaningful regional analysis can be performed. Future editions of this survey may enable us to confirm whether this perceived difference is an ongoing trend, especially if specific policy landscapes can be more firmly coupled to attitudes around research information management.

On the other hand, it was not surprising to find that "Recording institutional research facilities and their use" was not an important driver for the majority of respondents. The survey development team included this option because it is believed to be an emerging area of RIM practice, desirable for the future linking of research projects to grants, publications, datasets, and the equipment used to support the research. Aware of the costs involved in the development and purchase of research equipment, research funders these days are keen to explore sharing equipment and research facilities across institutions and within the industry.[29] It will be interesting to see if we observe changes in relevance in future survey efforts.

Regional differences

We also saw regional drivers for RIM adoption, although not always the ones we expected to see. For example, a comparatively higher percentage of institutions in the US considered "supporting expertise discovery" an extremely important reason for pursuing RIM. This in itself did not surprise us. Many in the US were first introduced to RIM systems as Research Networking Systems (RNS). Profiles RNS, open source software developed by Harvard Catalyst, was one of the first examples of a RIM system to gain prominence in the US, and emphasized the delivery of a public portal to support social networking and expertise discovery.[30] However, we believe the percentage would have been even higher for the US if our sample had been more representative of RIM systems in the US, in particular of the Profiles RNS and VIVO communities. Future editions of this survey will seek to fill that gap to confirm or correct our assumption.

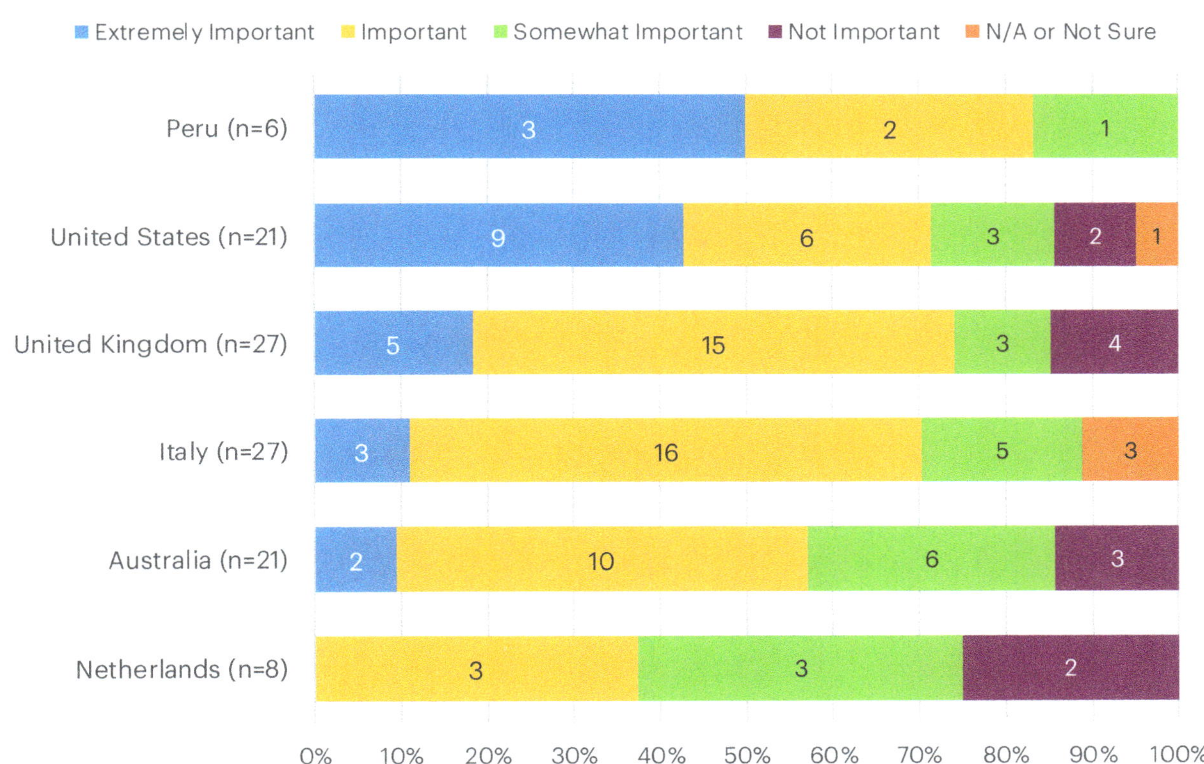

Importance of Supporting Expertise Discovery
Extremely Important
Important
Somewhat Important
Not Important
N/A or Not Sure
Peru (n=6)
3
2
1
United States (n=21)
9
6
3
2
1
United Kingdom (n=27)
5
15
3
4
Italy (n=27)
3
16
5
3
Australia (n=21)
2
10
6
3
Netherlands (n=8)
3
3
2
0%
10%
20%
30%
40%
50%
60%
70%
80%
90%
100%

FIGURE 13. Importance of Supporting Expertise Discovery for institutions with a live RIM system, with country subdivisions. (n=222).

In contrast, not a single institution in the Netherlands considered "Supporting expertise discovery" extremely important. This is likely because the Dutch have a nationally aggregated portal, NARCIS, for supporting group-scale aggregation and discovery of Dutch expertise and research, making it less urgent to consider the creation of local institutional expertise portals, in relation to other RIM activities.[31]

More regional differences are revealed in the deeper analysis of individual RIM uses below.

IMPORTANT FUNCTIONS OF RIM

Anticipating that institutions may find multiple uses for RIM metadata, services, or workflows once a system is implemented, we asked respondents to identify *all* of the functions of RIM that are important to their institution. Overall, a large majority of institutions cited "Registry of institutional research outputs" as an important function, with 77% citing this as an extremely important function. Internal reporting, while not cited as extremely important by as many institutions, was nonetheless cited as extremely important, important, or somewhat important by 98% of respondents.

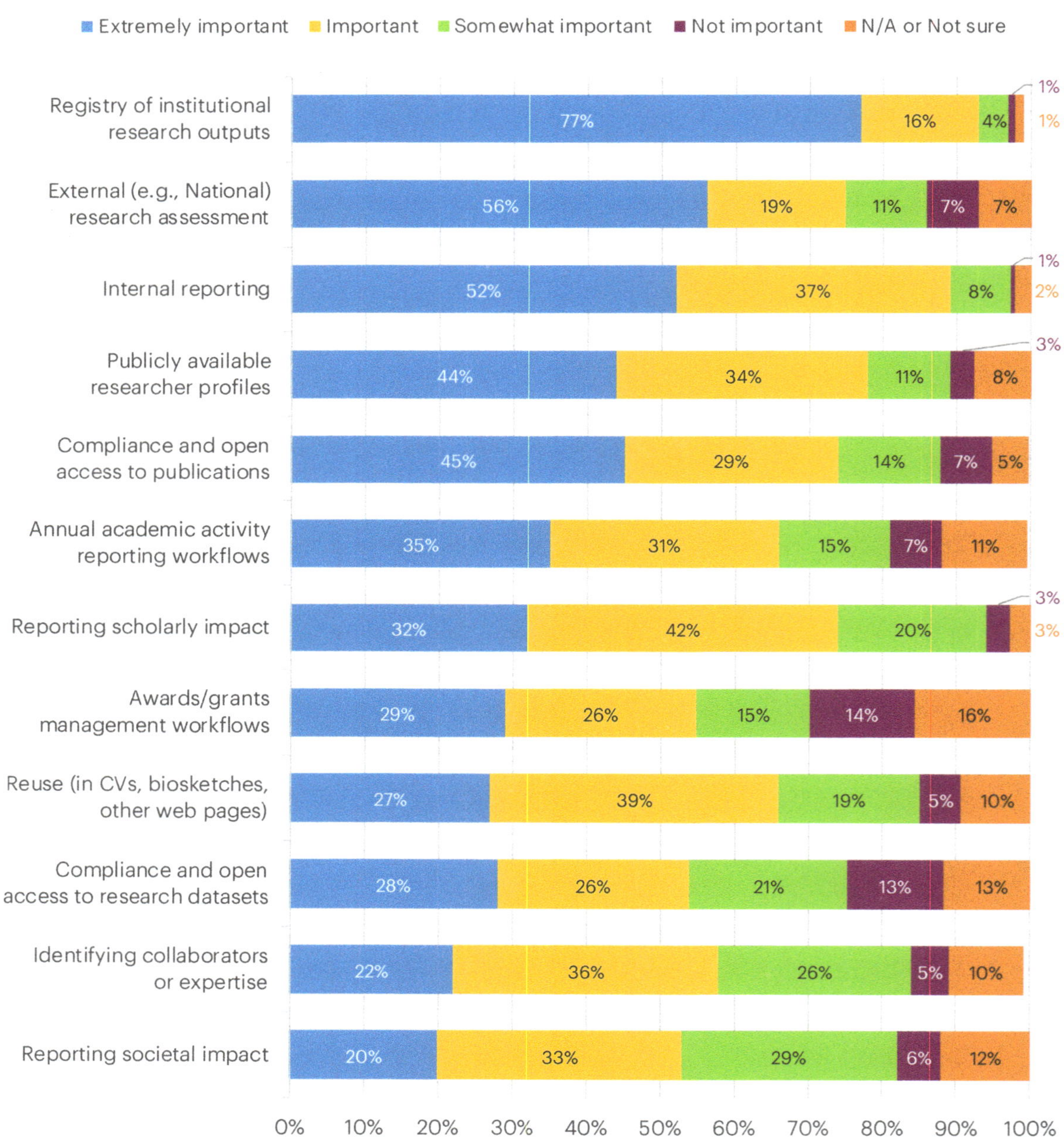

Important Functions of RIM (n=203)
Base: Institutions with a *live RIM system*
Extremely important
Important
Somewhat important
Not important
N/A or Not sure
Registry of institutional research outputs
77%
16%
4%
1%
1%
External (e.g., National) research assessment
56%
19%
11%
7%
7%
Internal reporting
52%
37%
8%
1%
2%
Publicly available researcher profiles
44%
34%
11%
3%
8%
Compliance and open access to publications
45%
29%
14%
7%
5%
Annual academic activity reporting workflows
35%
31%
15%
7%
11%
Reporting scholarly impact
32%
42%
20%
3%
3%
Awards/grants management workflows
29%
26%
15%
14%
16%
Reuse (in CVs, biosketches, other web pages)
27%
39%
19%
5%
10%
Compliance and open access to research datasets
28%
26%
21%
13%
13%
Identifying collaborators or expertise
22%
36%
26%
5%
10%
Reporting societal impact
20%
33%
29%
6%
12%
0%
10%
20%
30%
40%
50%
60%
70%
80%
90%
100%

FIGURE 14. Functions of RIM considered important by institutions with a live RIM system, ranked by percentage of institutions considering a function "extremely important."

We also asked this question of institutions in the process of implementing RIM systems, and their responses do not differ much from institutions with a live RIM system; it is noteworthy, however, that external research assessment functions seem to play a less crucial role than for institutions with a RIM system already in production. This is congruent with the suggestion above that more institutions in countries not subject to national reporting mandates may now be implementing RIM systems.

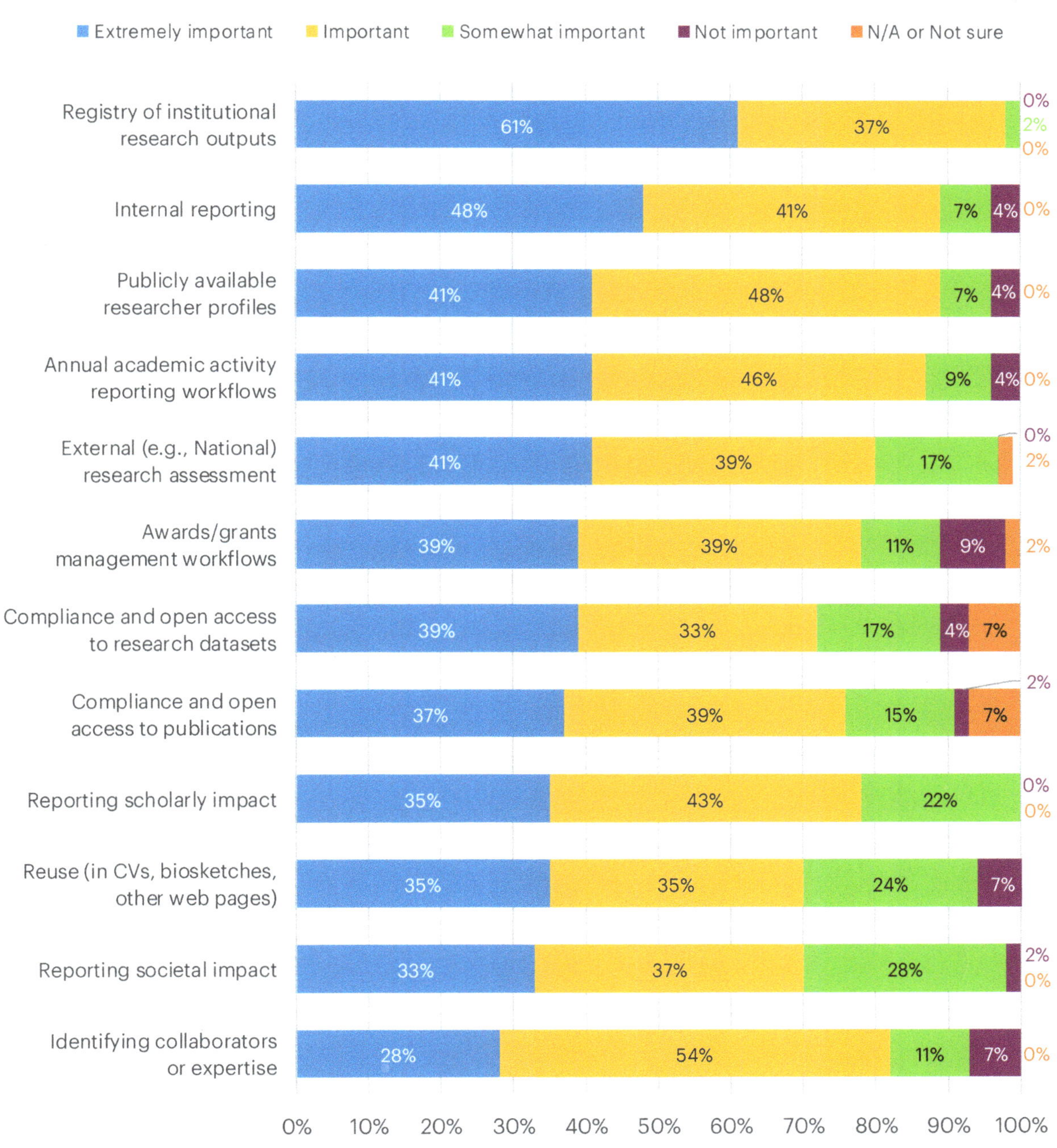

Important Functions of RIM (n=46)
Base: Institutions in process of implementing RIM system
Extremely important
Important
Somewhat important
Not important
N/A or Not sure
Registry of institutional research outputs
61%
37%
0%
2%
0%
Internal reporting
48%
41%
7%
4%
0%
Publicly available researcher profiles
41%
48%
7%
4%
0%
Annual academic activity reporting workflows
41%
46%
9%
4%
0%
External (e.g., National) research assessment
41%
39%
17%
0%
2%
Awards/grants management workflows
39%
39%
11%
9%
2%
Compliance and open access to research datasets
39%
33%
17%
4%
7%
Compliance and open access to publications
37%
39%
15%
2%
7%
Reporting scholarly impact
35%
43%
22%
0%
0%
Reuse (in CVs, biosketches, other web pages)
35%
35%
24%
7%
Reporting societal impact
33%
37%
28%
2%
0%
Identifying collaborators or expertise
28%
54%
11%
7%
0%
0%
10%
20%
30%
40%
50%
60%
70%
80%
90%
100%

FIGURE 15. Functions of RIM considered important by institutions implementing RIM systems, ranked by percentage of institutions considering a function "extremely important."

Regional differences

Regional differences can be observed for the relevance of some functions, many of which will be discussed in more detail below.

There is a notable regional difference regarding "Award/grant management workflows." Grants and awards management systems provide information about extramural research support. Awards management workflows may be closely integrated with other RIM functionality or exist completely separately. Few institutions in the US or the Netherlands reported that "Awards/grants management workflows" were an extremely important or important RIM function, as did fewer than half of the institutions in Italy. Institutions in Australia and Peru, however, reported that the function was extremely important or important at a much higher rate, which suggests the greater integration of awards management workflows within research information management practices in some regions.[32]

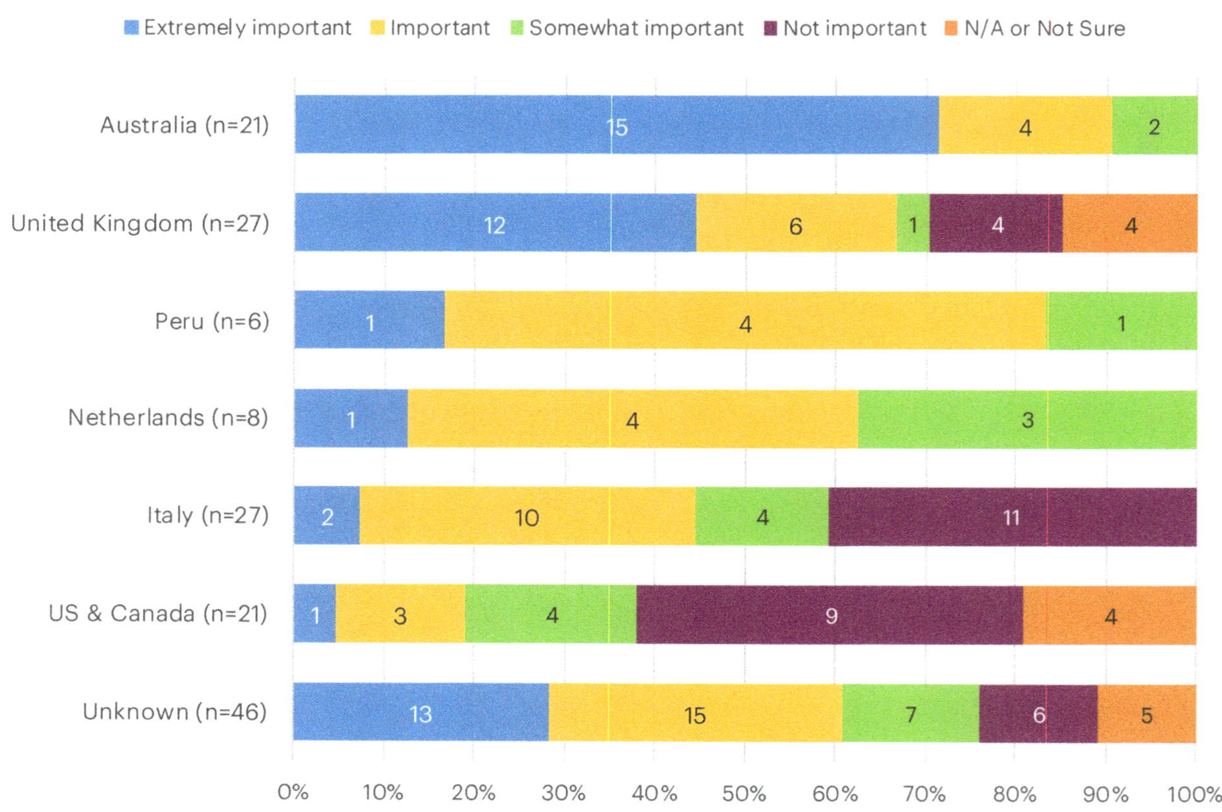
Importance of Award/Grant Management Workflows
Extremely important
Important
Somewhat important
Not important
N/A or Not Sure
Australia (n=21)
15
4
2
United Kingdom (n=27)
12
6
1
4
4
Peru (n=6)
1
4
1
Netherlands (n=8)
1
4
3
Italy (n=27)
2
10
4
11
US & Canada (n=21)
1
3
4
9
4
Unknown (n=46)
13
15
7
6
5
0%
10%
20%
30%
40%
50%
60%
70%
80%
90%
100%

FIGURE 16. Importance of Award/Grant Management Workflows for institutions with a live RIM system.

IMPORTANCE OF INCENTIVES FOR RESEARCHERS TO USE RIM SYSTEMS

We also asked survey respondents to reflect on the question "How important are the following incentives for scholars and researchers to use the RIM system(s) at your institution?"

Among institutions with a live RIM system, more than three-quarters responded that publicly sharing information about research and scholarship (88%) and that having a "national, funder, institutional, and department mandate" (86%) were believed to be among the most important incentives for researchers to use RIM systems.

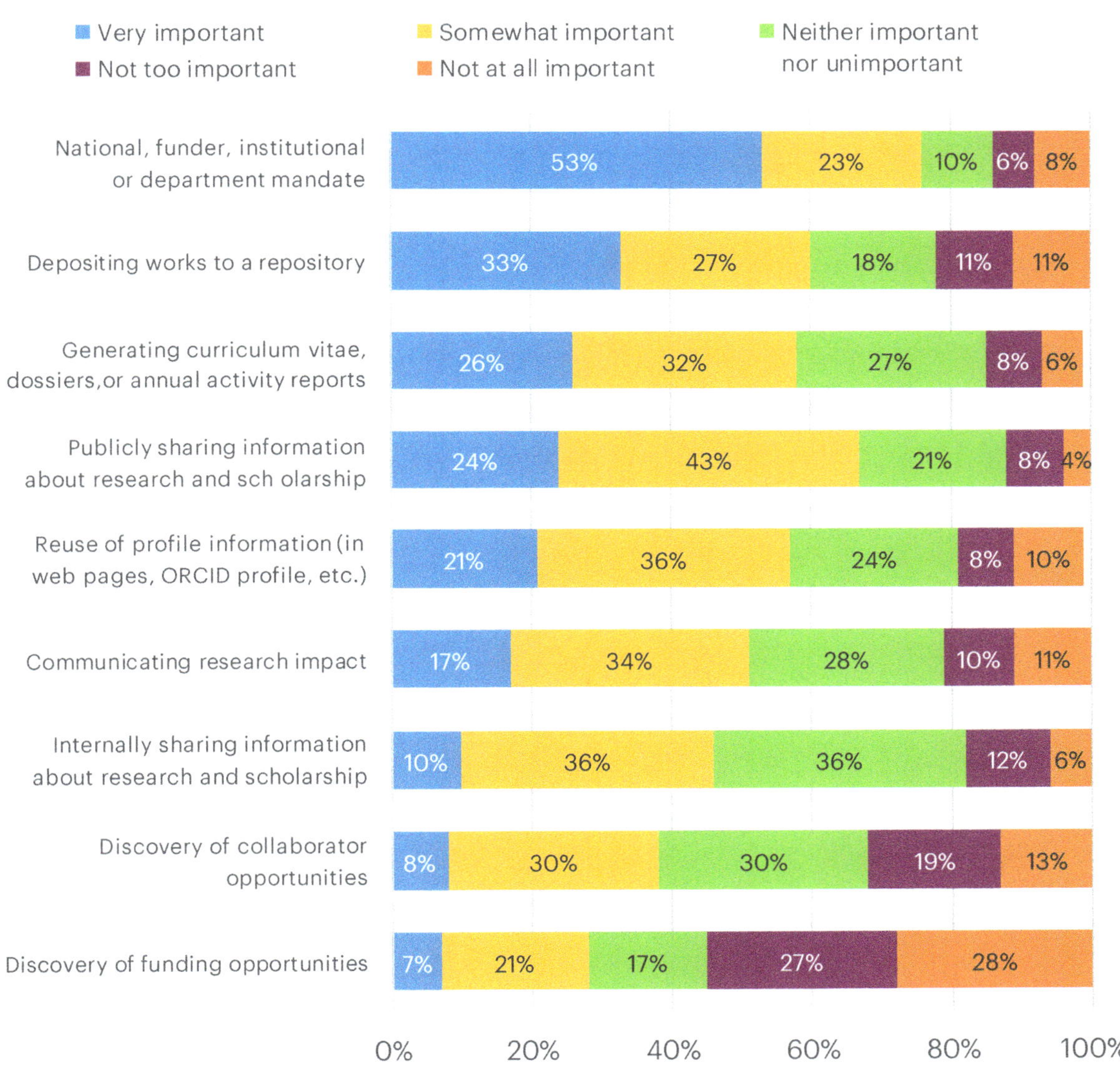

Importance of Incentives for Researchers to Use RIM System (n=154)
Very important
Somewhat important
Neither important nor unimportant
Not too important
Not at all important
National, funder, institutional or department mandate
53%
23%
10%
6%
8%
Depositing works to a repository
33%
27%
18%
11%
11%
Generating curriculum vitae, dossiers,or annual activity reports
26%
32%
27%
8%
6%
Publicly sharing information about research and sch olarship
24%
43%
21%
8%
4%
Reuse of profile information (in web pages, ORCID profile, etc.)
21%
36%
24%
8%
10%
Communicating research impact
17%
34%
28%
10%
11%
Internally sharing information about research and scholarship
10%
36%
36%
12%
6%
Discovery of collaborator opportunities
8%
30%
30%
19%
13%
Discovery of funding opportunities
7%
21%
17%
27%
28%
0%
20%
40%
60%
80%
100%

FIGURE 17. Incentives for researchers considered important by institutions with a live RIM system, ranked by percentage of institutions considering an incentive "Very important."

Among the incentives for scholars and researchers believed to be important at institutions currently implementing RIM systems, "Reuse of profile information," "Communicating research impact," and "Publicly sharing information about research and scholarship" are listed at the top.

Note that responses are delivered from the perspective of those completing the survey rather than the researchers themselves; asking researchers about their incentives might have produced a different result.

Furthermore, some institutions cannot or do not support a direct researcher user interface. In those cases, administrative staff complete RIM functions for researchers. For example, survey respondents commented:

> "All are important to extremely important but researchers aren't incentivised to us[e] our system because it is incredibly difficult to use and not fi[t] for purpose." **(Australia)**
>
> "Our RIM is a 'closed' system in that only administrative staff have access. Scholars do not have access as a general rule." **(Australia)**
>
> "We do not ask our scholars to use the RIS, the information is curated by the research office." **(UK)**

RELEVANT RIM AREAS: ANALYSIS AND DISCUSSION

As mentioned above, we asked survey respondents to respond to three related lines of questions related to research information management:

- Why did your institution pursue RIM activities? **(Reasons for pursuing RIM activities)**
- Which RIM functions are important to your institution? **(RIM functions)**
- How important are specific incentives for scholars and researchers to use the RIM system(s) at your institution? **(Researcher incentives for using RIM systems)**

In the section below, we provide an in-depth analysis of three selected RIM areas represented in all three question sets:

1. Managing annual academic activity reporting with related activities and workflows, such as generating annual activity reports or internal sharing of information about research activities
2. Supporting institutional compliance with internal or external mandates concerning performance or open access to publications and datasets
3. Supporting institutional reputation and strategic decision making by registering research outputs and activities and communicating and reporting on impact in a number of ways

Managing annual academic activity reporting

Reasons for pursuing RIM activities	RIM functions	Researcher incentives for using RIM systems
Managing annual academic activity reporting	Annual academic activity reporting workflows	Generating CVs, dossiers, or annual activity reports Internally sharing information about research and scholarship

Annual activity reporting relates to the process of gathering and reporting a summary of publication, presentation, grant, teaching, and other academic activities, predominantly for yearly review and/or for promotion and tenure.

As indicated above, "Managing annual academic activity reporting" ranks first as the most important reason for pursuing RIM activities among institutions with a live RIM system; more than half ranked it as an extremely important **reason for pursuing RIM activities**, and 86% think of it as extremely important or important. While the majority of respondents also indicated that annual activity reporting was at least an important **function of RIM** and an important perceived **incentive for researchers**, percentages are lower for both.

This may be a good example of a RIM area that became slightly less important to institutions (and potentially their researchers) once the system was available than when pursuing that system.

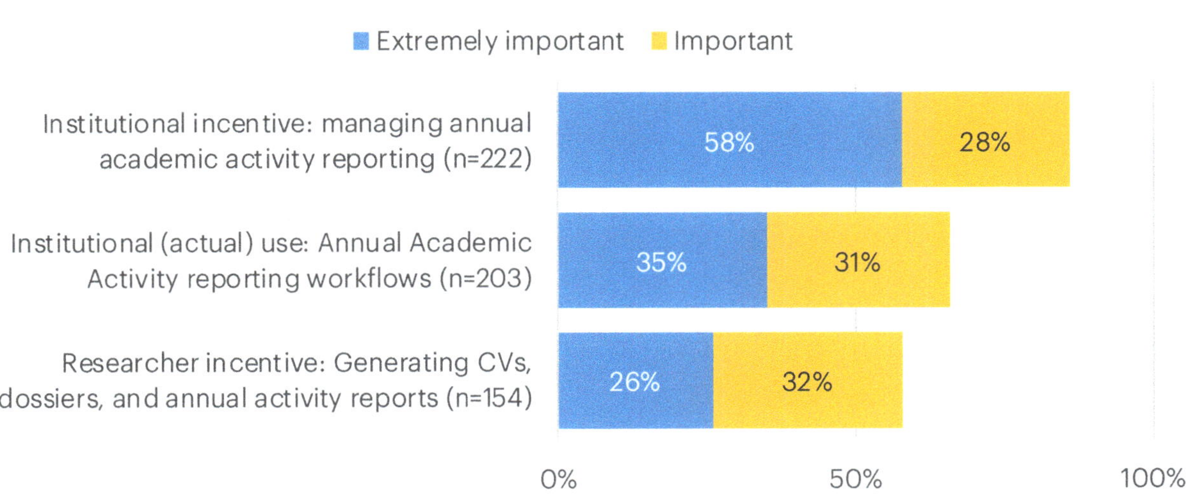

Annual Activity Reporting
Extremely important
Important
Institutional incentive: managing annual academic activity reporting (n=222)
58%
28%
Institutional (actual) use: Annual Academic Activity reporting workflows (n=203)
35%
31%
Researcher incentive: Generating CVs, dossiers, and annual activity reports (n=154)
26%
32%
0%
50%
100%

FIGURE 18. Summary of institutional incentives, RIM functions, and perceived researcher incentives for Annual Activity Reporting for institutions with a live RIM system.

Supporting institutional compliance

Reasons for pursuing RIM activities	RIM functions	Researcher incentives for using RIM systems
Supporting institutional compliance	External research assessment Compliance and open access to publications Compliance and open access to research datasets	National, funder, institutional, or department mandate Depositing works to a repository

Institutional compliance may mean different things from one country or institution to another, and may relate to satisfying mandates requiring research assessment reporting, open access, or research data management. It may even be overlapping, such as in the UK, where research assessment criteria establish that in order for a research output to be eligible for its consideration for the research assessment exercise, it must be open access. While some countries have uniform guidelines and requirements, others have no national requirements. Compliance might also refer to individual funder requirements or to local institutional policies.

Given the relevance of these compliance policies where available, it is not surprising that 53% of institutions with a live RIM system ranked "Supporting institutional compliance" as an extremely important **reason for pursuing RIM** activities.

When considering the importance of compliance to researchers, more than half of respondents indicated that they perceived national, funder, institutional, or department mandates to be extremely important **incentives to researchers for using a RIM system**—a much higher percentage than for "Depositing works to a repository" (33%). As one US respondent stated,

> "[Researchers are] Incentivized by desire to obtain funding for their research. The RIM system features are not the incentive they are the tools for obtaining funding."
> **(US)**

RIM systems may be used to support compliance in three main areas:

- External research assessment
- Open access to publications
- Open access to research datasets

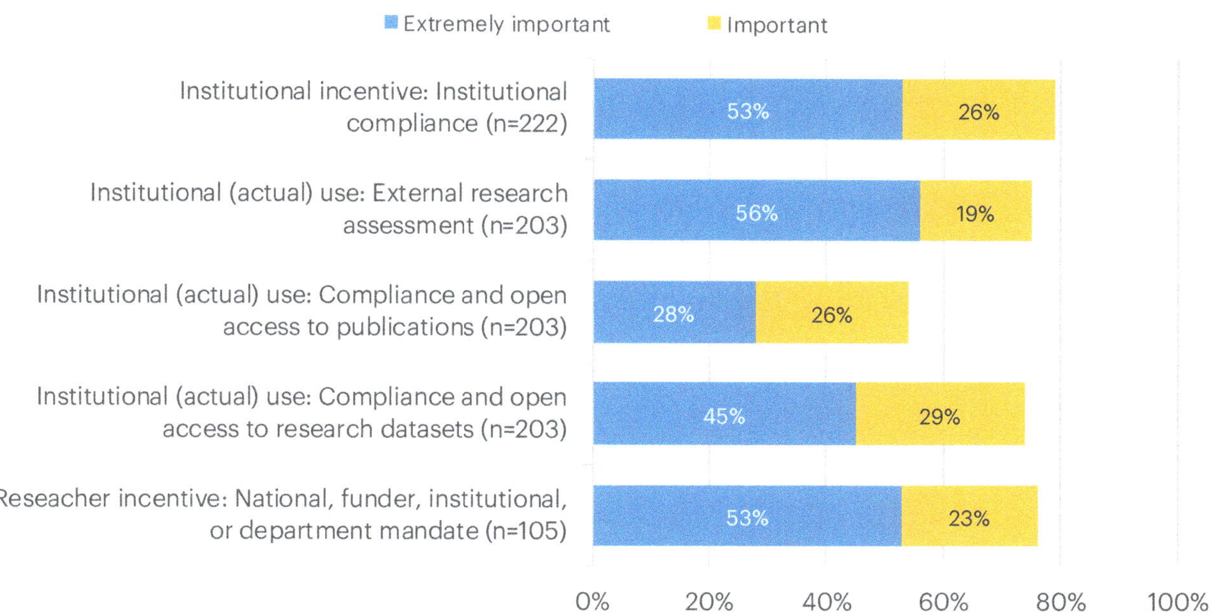
Institutional Compliance
Extremely important
Important
Institutional incentive: Institutional compliance (n=222)
53%
26%
Institutional (actual) use: External research assessment (n=203)
56%
19%
Institutional (actual) use: Compliance and open access to publications (n=203)
28%
26%
Institutional (actual) use: Compliance and open access to research datasets (n=203)
45%
29%
Reseacher incentive: National, funder, institutional, or department mandate (n=105)
53%
23%
0%
20%
40%
60%
80%
100%

FIGURE 19. Summary of institutional incentives, RIM functions, and perceived researcher incentives for Institutional Compliance for institutions with a live RIM system.

External research assessment

This is an area in which regional differences play a prominent role. For example, nearly all of the respondents from the UK and Australia indicated that "External research assessment" was an extremely important or important[33] **function of RIM**, which is not surprising given that national research assessment exercises are in place in both countries, while more than half of US respondents indicated that this function was not important or not applicable (figure 20), which is not surprising given the differences in research funders' policies, described in the introduction to this report. One Australian respondent noted in the comments:

> "Compliance with government regulations is the main driver behind RIM activities." **(Australia)**

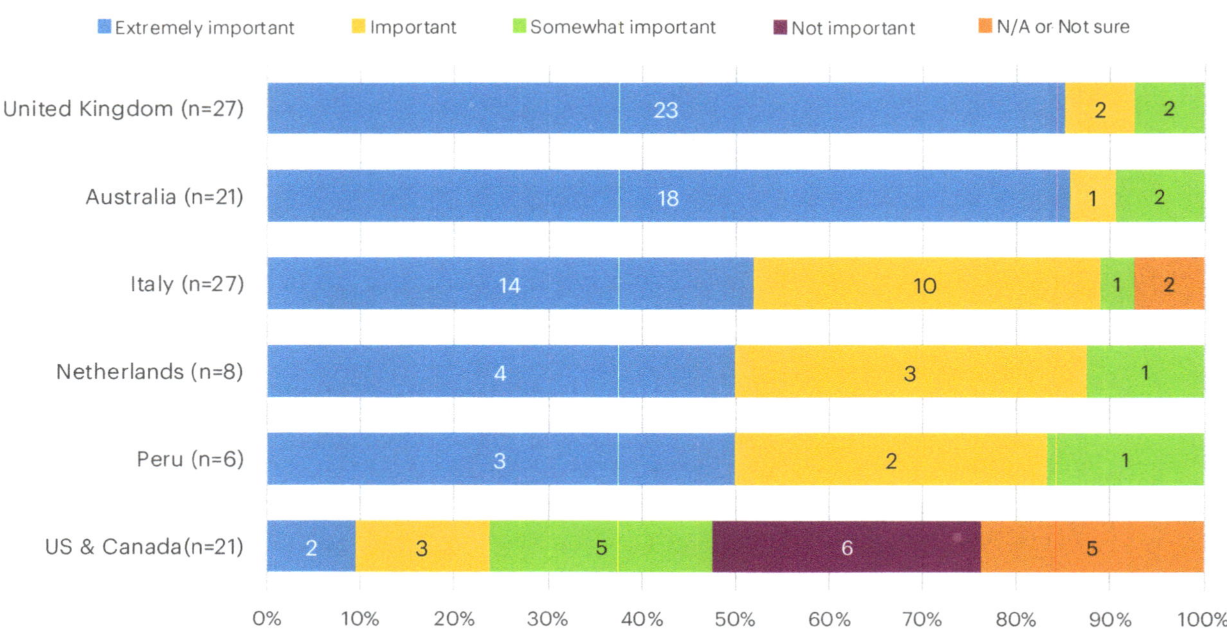
Importance of External Research Assessment Workflows
Extremely important
Important
Somewhat important
Not important
N/A or Not sure
United Kingdom (n=27)
23
2
2
Australia (n=21)
18
1
2
Italy (n=27)
14
10
1
2
Netherlands (n=8)
4
3
1
Peru (n=6)
3
2
1
US & Canada(n=21)
2
3
5
6
5
0%
10%
20%
30%
40%
50%
60%
70%
80%
90%
100%

FIGURE 20. Importance of RIM function "External Research Assessment" by country for institutions with a live RIM system.

Open access to publications

We asked about compliance and open access to two different kinds of research outputs: publications and datasets. Respondents felt that **RIM functions** supporting compliance and open access to publications were very similar in importance to functions supporting compliance with external research assessment, but considered compliance with research data management policies to be less important.

Importance of Compliance and Open Access to Publications

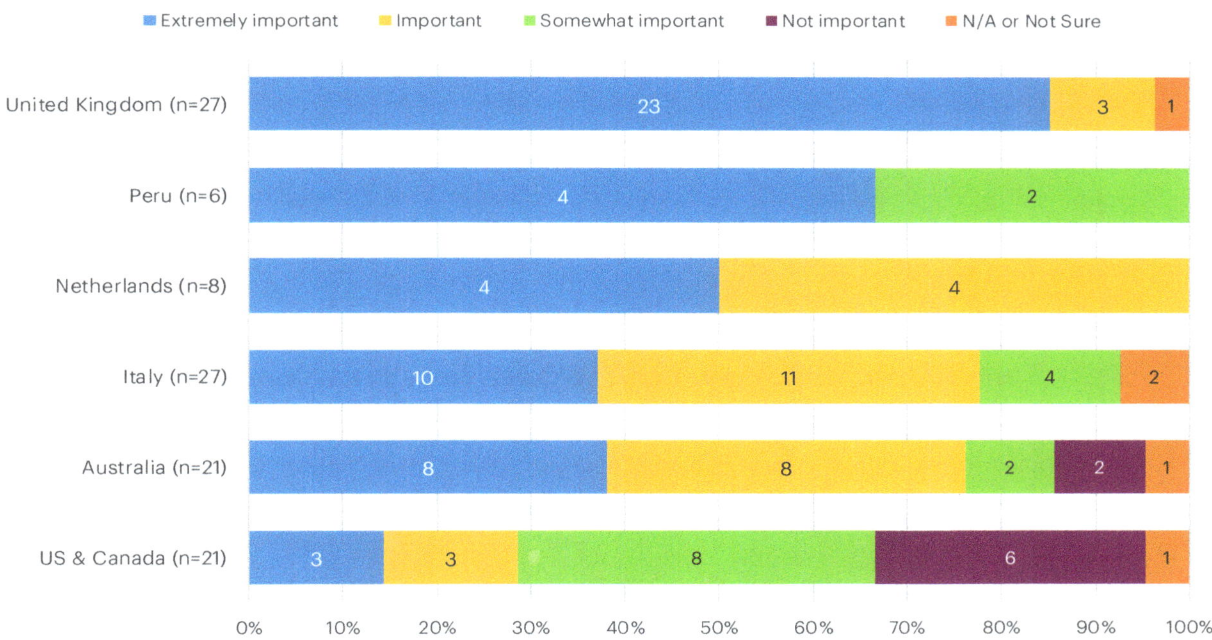

Extremely important
Important
Somewhat important
Not important
N/A or Not Sure
United Kingdom (n=27)
Peru (n=6)
Netherlands (n=8)
Italy (n=27)
Australia (n=21)
US & Canada (n=21)
23
3
1
4
2
4
4
10
11
4
2
8
8
2
2
1
3
3
8
6
1
0%
10%
20%
30%
40%
50%
60%
70%
80%
90%
100%

FIGURE 21. Importance of RIM function "Compliance and Open Access to Publications," grouped by country for institutions with a live RIM system.

"Compliance and open access to publications" was an extremely important or important **function of RIM** to the majority of responding institutions in all countries except the US. This correlates to the recent enactment of open access mandates by scores of funders, research organizations, and national and regional bodies.

In stark contrast, the US responses indicate less importance placed on **RIM functions** supporting open access compliance. While the 2013 policy memorandum from the US White House Office of Science and Technology similarly required the public availability of federally funded research, it is the responsibility of the researchers seeking federal funding, rather than the institutions, to comply; institutions do not need to track or report on their levels of compliance.[34]

Open access to research datasets

In contrast to "Compliance and open access to publications," far fewer institutions responded that open access to research datasets was an extremely important **function of RIM**. The differences in these responses may be credited to the relative maturity of policies aimed to make research outputs—initially publications and, only more recently, research datasets—publicly and openly available. Only institutions in Peru indicated that compliance with policies for open access to datasets was even more important for their institutional RIM strategies than compliance with open access policies regarding publications. Of respondents from the UK, 82% rated this as important or extremely important. While this is lower than the rating for publications, as compliance for datasets is not linked to the research assessment exercise, it is still high and reflects the importance of open data policies for UK research funders.

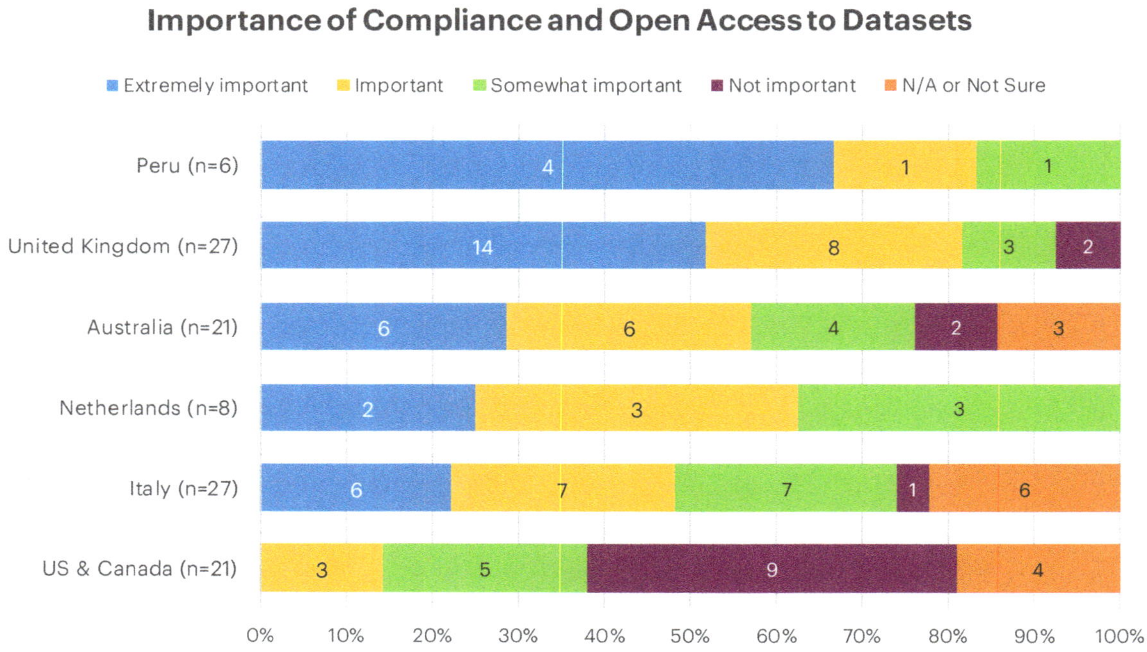

Importance of Compliance and Open Access to Datasets
Extremely important
Important
Somewhat important
Not important
N/A or Not Sure
Peru (n=6)
4
1
1
United Kingdom (n=27)
14
8
3
2
Australia (n=21)
6
6
4
2
3
Netherlands (n=8)
2
3
3
Italy (n=27)
6
7
7
1
6
US & Canada (n=21)
3
5
9
4
0%
10%
20%
30%
40%
50%
60%
70%
80%
90%
100%

FIGURE 22. Importance of RIM function "Compliance and Open Access to Datasets," grouped by country for institutions with a live RIM system.

Supporting institutional reputation and strategic decision making

Reasons for pursuing RIM activities	RIM functions	Researcher incentives for using RIM systems
Supporting institutional reputation and strategic decision making	Registry of institutional research outputs Internal reporting Reporting scholarly impact Reporting societal impact	Communicating research impact

"Supporting institutional reputation and strategic decision making" has been indicated as an extremely important or important **reason for pursuing RIM activities** by 81% of respondents. This objective is supported by a number of **RIM functions** potentially relevant in this context:

- Registry of institutional research outputs (to enhance institutional reputation)
- Internal reporting (for strategic decision making purposes)
- Reporting scholarly and societal impact (for reputation management)

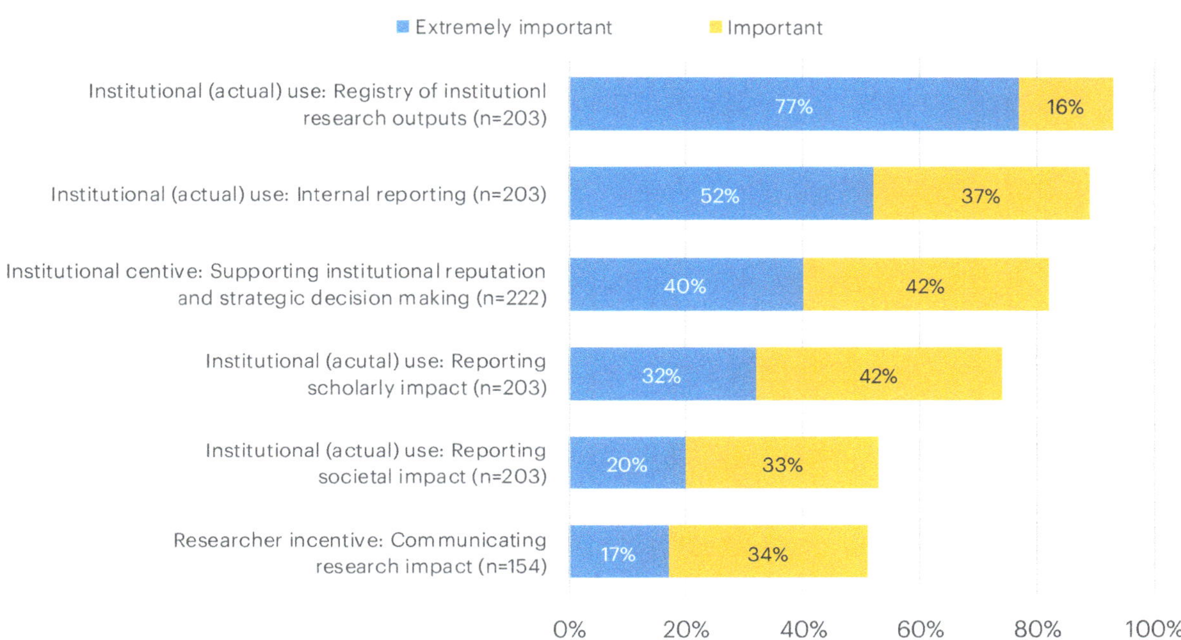
Supporting Institutional Reputation and Strategic Decision Making
Extremely important
Important
Institutional (actual) use: Registry of institutionl research outputs (n=203)
77%
16%
Institutional (actual) use: Internal reporting (n=203)
52%
37%
Institutional centive: Supporting institutional reputation and strategic decision making (n=222)
40%
42%
Institutional (acutal) use: Reporting scholarly impact (n=203)
32%
42%
Institutional (actual) use: Reporting societal impact (n=203)
20%
33%
Researcher incentive: Communicating research impact (n=154)
17%
34%
0%
20%
40%
60%
80%
100%

FIGURE 23. Summary of institutional incentives, RIM functions, and perceived researcher incentives for Supporting Institutional Reputation and Strategic Decision Making for institutions with a live RIM system.

The responses concerning the **RIM function** "Registry of institutional research outputs" were the most striking. In aggregate, this function ranked of highest importance among all RIM functions. All respondents in all countries—except the US—indicated that function was either extremely important or important. In contrast, only half of US respondents reported that the function was extremely important; a few indicated that the function was only somewhat important or even not important at all.

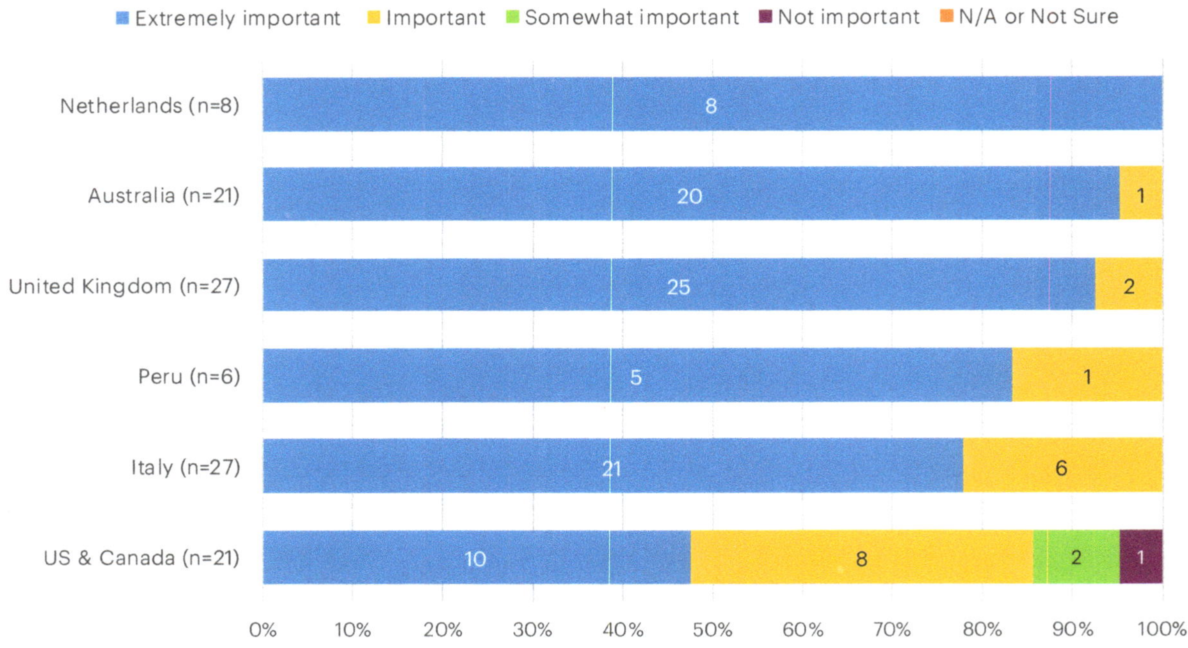
Importance of RIM System as Registry of Institutional Research Outputs
Extremely important
Important
Somewhat important
Not important
N/A or Not Sure
Netherlands (n=8)
Australia (n=21)
United Kingdom (n=27)
Peru (n=6)
Italy (n=27)
US & Canada (n=21)
8
20
1
25
2
5
1
21
6
10
8
2
1
0%
10%
20%
30%
40%
50%
60%
70%
80%
90%
100%

FIGURE 24. Importance of RIM function "Registry of Institutional Research Outputs," grouped by country for institutions with a live RIM system.

In comments, several respondents mentioned their institution's desire to have all research-related data in one place. For instance,

> "[The RIM serves] as a central source of research information for use by other systems, thereby reducing/eliminating duplication of efforts and research investment within the institution." **(US)**

> "In the US, institutions without RIMs rarely have easy ways of characterizing their institution's scholarly output beyond anecdote. When numbers are requested for internal or external use (e.g., rankings) staff are spending time dreaming up creative ways to get the requested data. A RIM allows the institution to have a system of record for research output that is well-understood and (assuming full adoption) useful across the organization." **(US)**

The **RIM function** "Internal reporting" was extremely important or important by 89% of the respondents with live RIM systems.

"[The RIM serves] as a central source of research information for use by other systems, thereby reducing/eliminating duplication of efforts and research investment within the institution." **(US)**

In comments, one respondent expressed the hope that they would make greater use of their RIM for internal reporting in the future:

> "Primarily our RIM instance is to save faculty time for annual reporting, and to acquire better publications metadata on faculty productivity." **(US)**

"We are interested in expanding further in the future to link publications to grants, grants to projects, projects to equipment, and equipment to datasets (etc. etc. etc.) to get a more holistic understanding of the research life-cycle at our institution." **(US)**

RIM functions related to scholarly and societal impact were rated as comparatively less important; congruently, "Communicating research impact" was perceived as a less important incentive for researchers if compared to other options. In comments, one respondent indicated that their RIM is used for measuring impact, not just counts:

> "Providing accurate data for evidence-based decision-making. Seeking to measure impact of research activities. Discovering networks for possible collaboration and opportunities for joint research projects." **(UK)**

But another reflected on the differences among stakeholders regarding what should be measured and reported:

> "There is a disconnect between scholars/researchers and Provost/Executive Team regarding impact. Scholars wish for the system to record every type of impact imaginable, but at present the Provost's office is not interested in impacts, only outputs." **(US)**

Judging from the current trends in RIM environments like the UK's, and mainly driven by research funders' policies, it's not hard to anticipate that these RIM functions related to scholarly and societal impact will gain relevance in the mid-term, as the measurement of impact as a RIM objective gains widespread acceptance. This is another aspect to be further analyzed in future iterations of this survey and in any follow-up activities that drill deeper into the data for specific geographic areas.

PERCEPTIONS OF RESEARCH INFORMATION MANAGEMENT SUCCESS

In order to explore the perceived success of current RIM activities, complementing our understanding of RIM system satisfaction levels as noted above, we asked respondents to indicate how successful their institution was in accomplishing the live RIM functions they considered extremely important or important, as described earlier in this report.

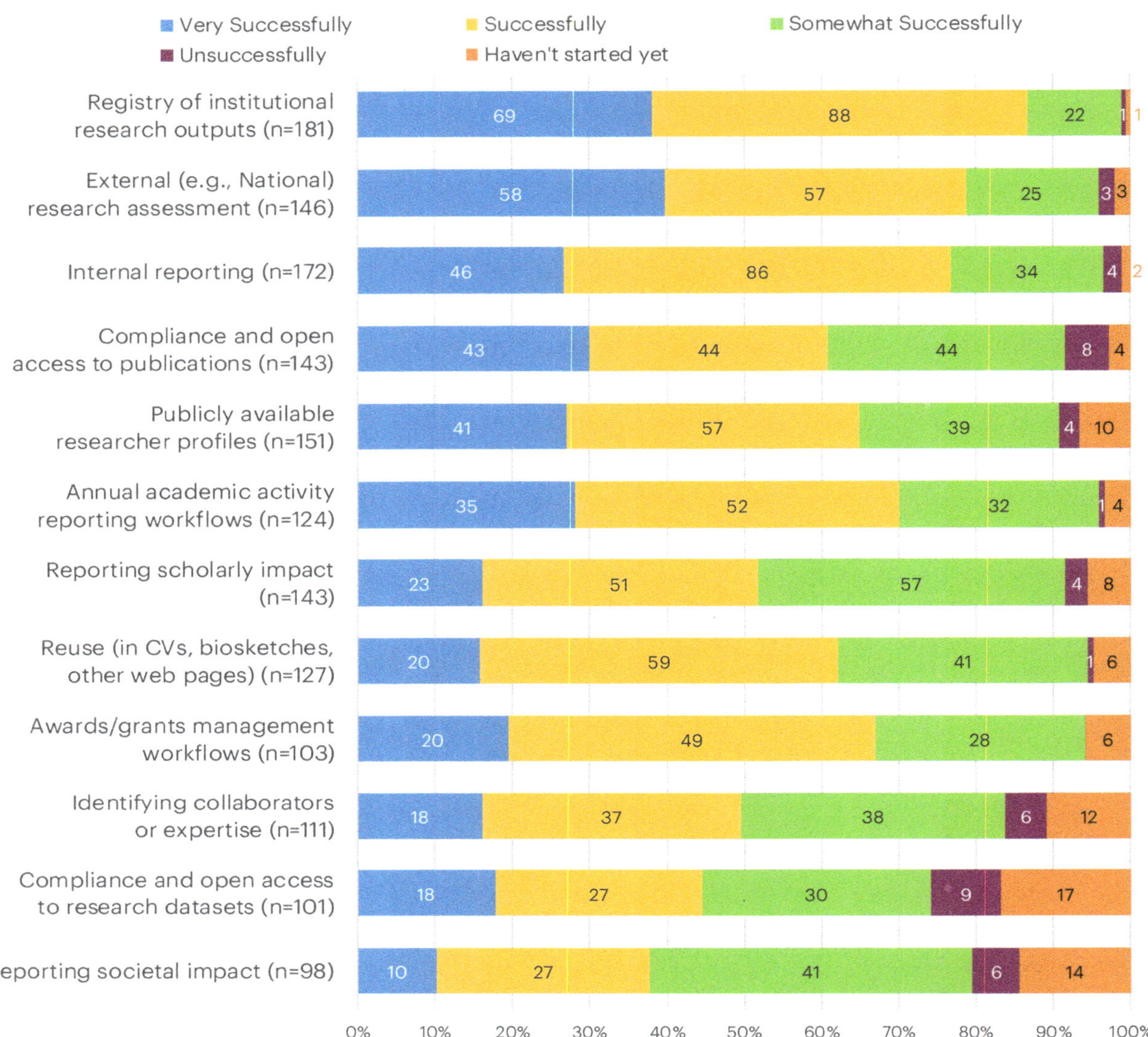
Success Levels for RIM Functions Seen as Extremely Important or Important
Very Successfully
Successfully
Somewhat Successfully
Unsuccessfully
Haven't started yet
Registry of institutional research outputs (n=181)
69
88
22
1
1
External (e.g., National) research assessment (n=146)
58
57
25
3
3
Internal reporting (n=172)
46
86
34
4
2
Compliance and open access to publications (n=143)
43
44
44
8
4
Publicly available researcher profiles (n=151)
41
57
39
4
10
Annual academic activity reporting workflows (n=124)
35
52
32
1
4
Reporting scholarly impact (n=143)
23
51
57
4
8
Reuse (in CVs, biosketches, other web pages) (n=127)
20
59
41
1
6
Awards/grants management workflows (n=103)
20
49
28
6
Identifying collaborators or expertise (n=111)
18
37
38
6
12
Compliance and open access to research datasets (n=101)
18
27
30
9
17
Reporting societal impact (n=98)
10
27
41
6
14
0%
10%
20%
30%
40%
50%
60%
70%
80%
90%
100%

FIGURE 25. Success levels for RIM functions seen as extremely important or important by institutions with live RIM instances.

Overall, for the functions that were of importance to the highest number of institutions—"Registry of institutional research output," "External research assessment," and "Internal reporting"—a large majority of respondents indicated they were very successfully or successfully performing the function.

Interestingly, for each function of RIM, there was at least one institution that had not yet started implementing, even though they consider it an important part of their RIM strategy. With the only exception of "Awards/grants management," for every function, at least one institution reported that they were unsuccessful in providing it. This was most striking for "Compliance and open access for datasets." About 10% of those institutions for which this was an extremely important or important function are not yet successfully performing in this area, which is not surprising, given that open access to datasets is still emerging in both policy and practice.

In general, we observe a correlation between perceived success of RIM functions and the longevity of practice.

SUMMARY: RIM INCENTIVES AND USES

> "A single system that collects different research related information of all faculty to form a single source of truth with validated information to facilitate the reuse of the information for different purposes to streamline the workflow and reduce the administrative burden of the faculty." (China)

A closer look at the incentives for pursuing RIM activities, the functions considered important, and the applications of RIM systems, reveals a diverse and complex ecosystem of practice.

National research assessment frameworks and open science policies were identified as key differentiators, strongly shaping priorities of RIM activities in those countries and regions where they exist. This is congruent with results from previous qualitative research that documented the impact of national research assessment frameworks and open access mandates, and how these have contributed to a growing need for institutional processes and interoperability to support scalable data collection and reporting, as well as improved and more convenient one-stop user interfaces for researchers.[35]

National research assessment frameworks and open science policies were identified as key differentiators, strongly shaping priorities of RIM activities in those countries and regions where they exist.

While these drivers are extremely significant in many locales, there are other dynamics at play. In certain regions, at least, other considerations are coming to the fore, including the need to improve services for researchers. In view of the disconnect between researcher and institutional needs regarding RIM and their respective use of RIM systems, this is an interesting development worth watching.

Some uses of RIM are still developing and can be expected to grow, such as fostering open access to datasets, which is currently not as strongly prioritized as open access to publications.

Finally, initial intention does not necessarily match actual use. Annual academic activity reporting may be an area where current priorities differ from the expectations that originally drove implementation.

Repositories and RIM

RIM systems, as mentioned above, have their roots in administrative efforts initially led by the campus research office. Institutional repositories (IRs), on the other hand, grew out of a need for institutions to support open access to their research outputs, primarily publications. This effort was usually led by the library. The fact that both RIM systems and IRs were involved in collecting information about publications at times led to a perception of "duplication of effort," and tension between research offices and libraries.

However, while RIM systems and IRs overlap in functionality, there are characteristic differences. The main purpose of collecting publications as part of RIM is to collect and validate institutional research outputs, in order to support any number of institutional functions, such as research assessment, strategic planning, or reuse. The main purpose of an IR is to facilitate open access and reuse of publications, and, increasingly, other types of research outputs. In other words, "From the CRIS perspective, publications are the result of projects and related institutional activities. From the IR point of view, publications are academic resources to be made available for reuse."[36]

The term *scholarly communications repository* is used here as an umbrella term to encompass traditional institutional repositories, mostly focused on open access to publications and repositories for other kinds of institutional outputs, in particular, research data and electronic theses and dissertations (ETDs). The term institutional repository is sometimes used more broadly to cover all of those, regardless of content type, whether combined or as separate systems; other terms used in this context are digital repositories, open access repositories, or simply repositories.

By including specific questions concerning scholarly communications repositories in this survey, our goal was to better understand the current state of interoperability and integration between RIM systems and different kinds of repositories in response to evolving policies, technologies, and practices. This is building on the previous CRIS/IR Survey Report published in 2016 by EUNIS and euroCRIS.

Institutions were asked:

- If their RIM system served as a *default* repository for one or more types of scholarly content
- If their RIM system *interoperated* with a standalone IR (for example, via a connector between DSpace and Pure)

USE OF THE RIM SYSTEM AS A DEFAULT REPOSITORY

Respondents were asked if their current RIM system serves as their default institutional repository, electronic thesis and dissertation (ETD) repository, and/or research data repository. By answering affirmatively to this question, the institution indicated it was using a RIM platform or system that also provides functionality usually associated with repositories, such as the ability to deposit publications for open access; this is to be distinguished from RIM systems that rely on a connector to support system-to-system *interoperability*, which was asked about in a separate question.

In aggregate, just over half (54%) of the respondents indicate their RIM system serves as their institutional repository, for over a third (37%) it serves as their ETD repository, and for a quarter (24%) as their research data repository.

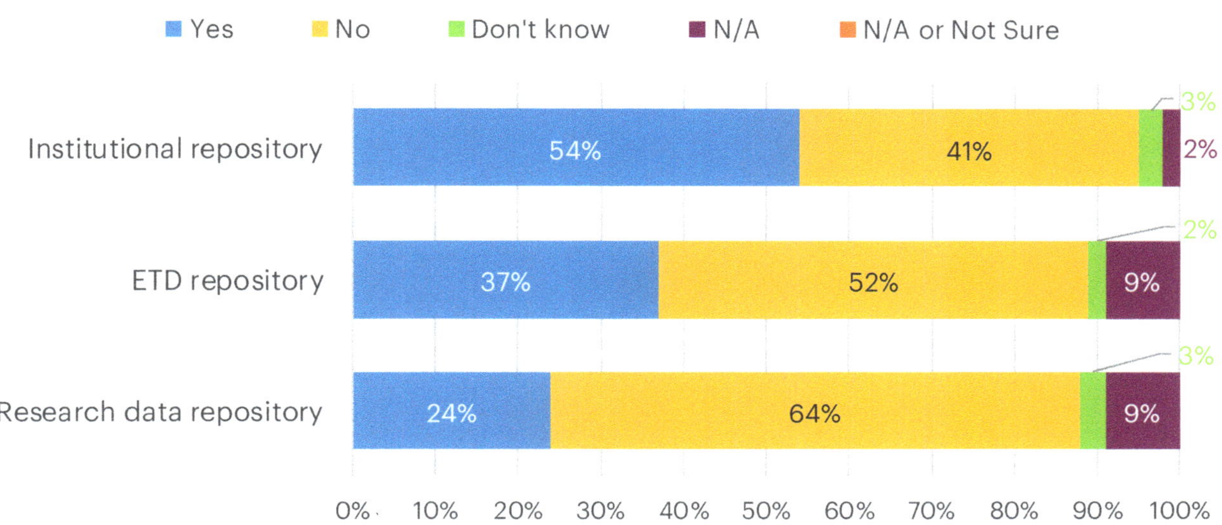

Does Your RIM System Serve as Your Default...
Yes
No
Don't know
N/A
N/A or Not Sure
Institutional repository
54%
41%
3%
2%
ETD repository
37%
52%
2%
9%
Research data repository
24%
64%
3%
9%
0%
10%
20%
30%
40%
50%
60%
70%
80%
90%
100%

FIGURE 26. Institutions with a live RIM platform reporting that their RIM system serves as their default institutional repository/ETD repository/research data repository.

There are some interesting regional differences suggested in figure 27. The adoption of RIM systems with IR functionality appears strongest in Europe, where RIM systems (usually called CRIS in this environment) have been in place longest. Nearly 70% (n=95) report using their CRIS as their default institutional repository, responses were particularly pronounced in Italy and the UK. A similar version of this question was asked in the EUNIS-euroCRIS survey in 2015, in which 18% of responding institutions (n=82 from 20 European countries) reported using an integrated platform for CRIS and IR functionalities.[37]

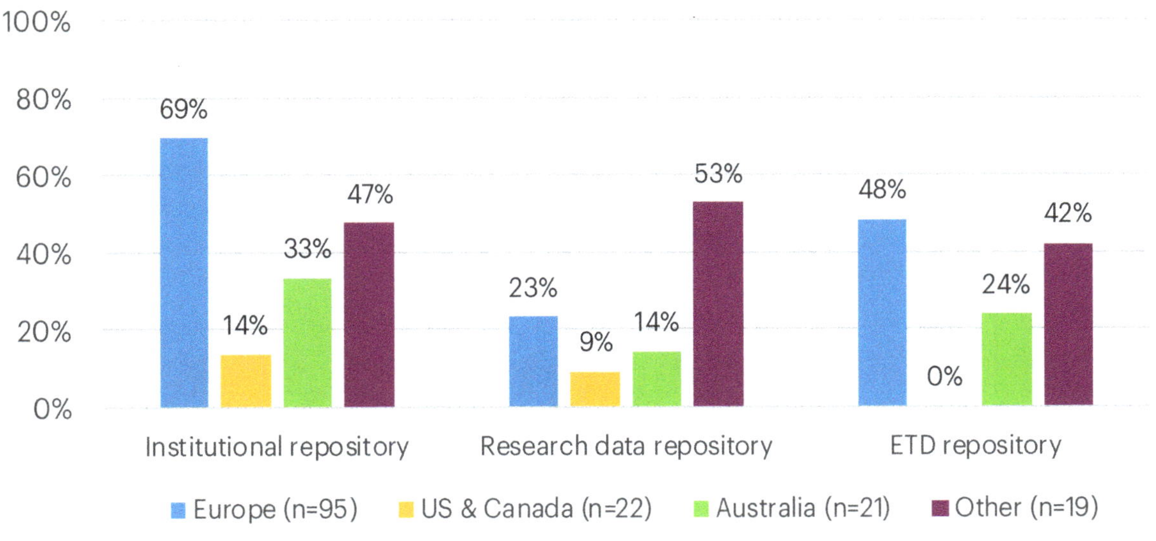

Does Your RIM System Serve as Your Default...
100%
80%
60%
40%
20%
0%
69%
14%
33%
47%
23%
9%
14%
53%
48%
0%
24%
42%
Institutional repository
Research data repository
ETD repository
Europe (n=95)
US & Canada (n=22)
Australia (n=21)
Other (n=19)

FIGURE 27. Institutions with a live RIM system reporting that their RIM system serves as their default institutional repository/ETD repository/research data repository, with regional subdivisions.

While this difference in percentages suggests growing adoption of cross-functional platforms in Europe, providing both RIM and IR functionality, this also may be due to changing perceptions. For instance, in the 2015 survey, Italian Cineca institutions responded that they had two interoperable systems (DSpace and IRIS), while in this 2017 survey, they uniformly responded that they have one single system fulfilling the roles of both RIM and IR (IRIS). Interestingly, the technology is largely unchanged, except for a move to cloud hosting; however, users' perspectives today are demonstrably different.

The use of the RIM system as a default research data repository is lower in Europe than for traditional institutional repository content, but at least one respondent expects this to be of growing importance for institutions, and particularly libraries:

> "Growing role of the library. . . is the support for Research Data archiving through the RIM (CRIS) system." **(Netherlands)**

Finally, the use of RIM systems as the default ETD repository is completely absent from US and Canadian institutions completing this survey, most likely reflecting the fact that graduate students are not usually included in North American RIM implementations, as discussed in the Institutional Populations Included in RIM section below.

Respondents also offered the following verbatim comments about their use of the RIM system as a repository:

> "As well as serving several other functions, our RIM is our repository and our tool for collating our submission to the REF (our national research assessment exercise). We couldn't operate without a system to support these functions and I can't envisage how other comparable universities might operate their REF submission without a RIM." **(UK)**

> "OMEGA-PSIR is a fully functional system of the class CRIS. It covers functionality of Institutional Repository, the first Repository that [institution] ever had. System allows reporting scientific achievements both internally and externally. Researchers' profiles can be used for generating CVs besause [sic] of the complete and comprehensive information stored in the knowledge base. By aggregating profiles of all employees of a given unit the system produces and visualizes a profile of the unit. It looks impressive." **(Poland)**

> [In response to question about "what prompted the migration?" from another RIM system]: "Needed something more automated and scalable that offered more services to researchers and integrated with our repository. Prior to this, research publication reporting was a separate system from OA deposit and scholarly impact metrics had to be collated from a range of bibliometric sources by librarians." **(Australia)**

> [In response to question about "what prompted the migration?"]: "We user [sic] DSpace simply as an institutional repository. We wanted a more comprehensive system, and chose Pure. The amount of data held in our DSpace instance was such that migration made more sense than maintaining two systems, and the connector between them." **(UK)**

> [In response to question about "what prompted the migration?]: "To choose a solution based on open source technology, on a modular architecture with an embedded Open repository." **(Italy)**

[In response to question, "Would you recommend your RIM system or not?]: "I would recommend a professional product, ideally open source and a combination of RIM and repository in one system." **(Austria; institution using a system developed in-house)**

INTEROPERABILITY BETWEEN FREE-STANDING RIM AND IR SYSTEMS

In a separate question, we asked respondents if their RIM system interoperated with other internal systems. They were given 13 options including:

- Institutional repository (e.g., via a connector between DSpace and Pure)
- Research data repository
- Electronic Thesis/Dissertation (ETD) repository

In aggregate, respondents indicated interoperability with stand-alone repositories being strongest for institutional repositories (43%) and lower for data repositories (16%) and ETD repositories (20%).

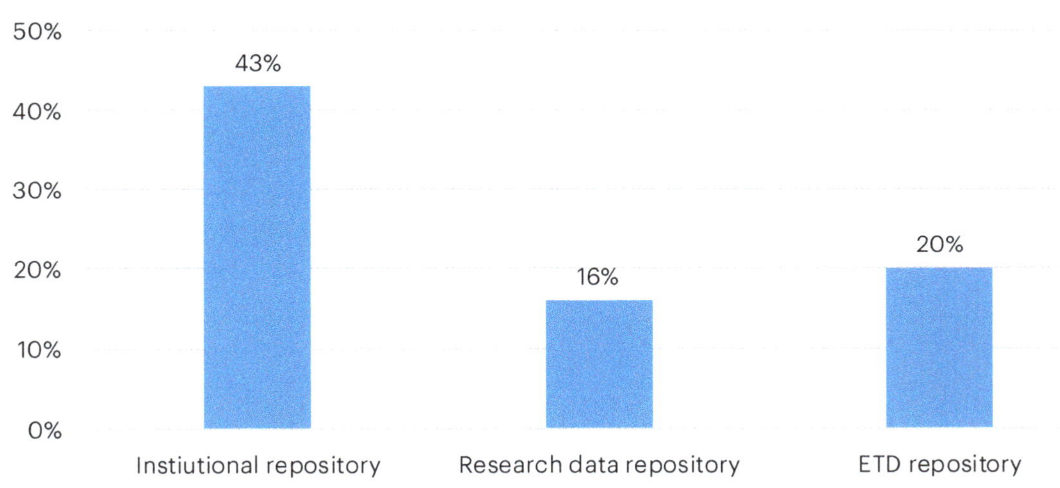

Interoperability Between RIM and Repository Systems (n=184)
50%
40%
30%
20%
10%
0%
43%
16%
20%
Instiutional repository
Research data repository
ETD repository

FIGURE 28. Institutions with live RIM instance reporting interoperability with institutional repository, research data repository, and ETD repository.

Interoperability with an ETD repository seems to play a stronger role with implementing institutions, where interoperability is mentioned more often (43%) than for institutional repositories (33%). On the other hand, for live institutions, interoperability with institutional repositories is far more common than with ETD repositories, potentially suggesting the inclusion of doctoral students within RIM systems at institutions currently implementing. Another relevant factor is the frequent institutional preference for keeping their theses and dissertations, which are often perceived to be their most significant research outputs as information providers, in institutional platforms that are not seen as at risk of being moved to the cloud.

With over 59% of respondents with a live RIM system implementation indicating an integrated RIM system-IR, and, at the same time, over 47% indicating interoperability with a stand-alone IR, it's not hard to notice that this, in aggregate, suggests that some institutions are using their RIM system as their default IR while also maintaining a connector with another institutional repository. Indeed, of those using their RIM as their default institutional repository, about a third also indicate interoperating with an institutional repository as another internal system. As suggested above, this could reflect some confusion by survey respondents, misunderstanding of the questions or the terminology used, or temporary maintenance of multiple systems before or during system migration. It could also be testimony to the fact that institutional repositories may serve multiple purposes, in potentially multiple instances, as articulated in a report published by CNI in 2017, "Many institutions described a situation where they have as many as five different platforms . . . that have characteristics of IRs. . . . "[38]

In open-ended comments, respondents offered thoughts on the importance of interoperability (sometimes called "integration" by respondents) between independent RIM and IR systems:

> "Symplectic is now our submission system into our institutional repository." **(Australia)**
>
> [In response to question about "what prompted the migration?"]: "It was no longer fit for purpose as a tool for our REF submission. We needed a system that allowed us to import bibliographic data from external sources, and that allowed us to integrate with ePrints (our institutional repository)." **(UK)**
>
> "Elements: was implemented to support our institutional Open access Policy and is integrated with our institutional repository. The tool itself and the intregation [sic] work fine, but fewer than 50% of our faculty engage with the system, and those who do don't upload much content because of the versioning issue." **(US)**

The need to implement both open access implementation workflows and wider RIM functions are giving rise to hybrid platforms that are simultaneously RIM systems and repositories.

There are some interesting regional distinctions for this question. Of European institutions, 42% (n=95) reported interoperability between a stand-alone IR and their CRIS, numbers that suggest a drop from the numbers reported in 2015 euroCRIS-EUNIS survey (n=86), in which 63% of respondents affirmed they had CRIS-IR interoperability in place.[39] **Overall, this result, in combination with the growing number of institutions reporting use of their RIM system as their default institutional repository, suggests a merging of RIM and IR functional categories.** The need to implement both open access implementation workflows and wider RIM functions are giving rise to hybrid platforms that are simultaneously RIM systems and repositories.[40] This change is occurring alongside changes in the open access publishing and data sharing requirements and social norms, and also with changes in stakeholder roles within the research ecosystem.[41,42]

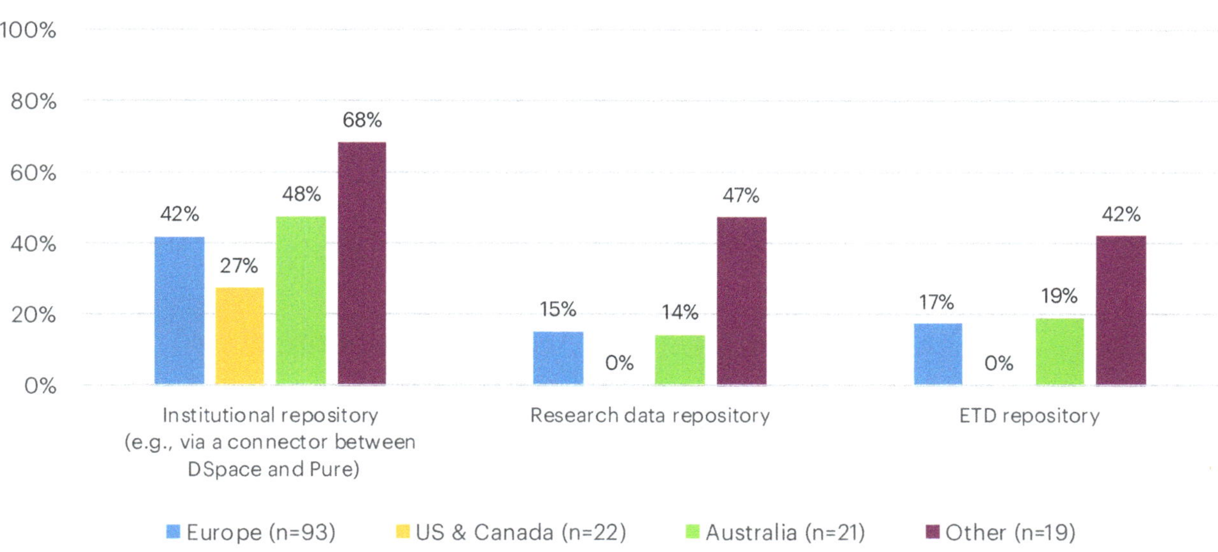
Which of the Following Internal Systems Interoperate with Your RIM System(s)?
100%
80%
60%
40%
20%
0%
42%
27%
48%
68%
15%
0%
14%
47%
17%
0%
19%
42%
Institutional repository (e.g., via a connector between DSpace and Pure)
Research data repository
ETD repository
Europe (n=93)
US & Canada (n=22)
Australia (n=21)
Other (n=19)

FIGURE 29. Institutions with live RIM system reporting internal interoperability with institutional repository, research data repository, and ETD repository, with regional subdivisions.

Further, even though our US and Canada sample is small, it suggests that North American use of the RIM system as a default repository, as well as the interoperability between siloed RIM and IR systems, lags behind Europe and other parts of the world. As discussed in the introduction, RIM practices developed earlier in Europe than elsewhere, and have had a longer period of maturity.

SUMMARY: REPOSITORIES AND RIM

Supporting open access to institutionally produced content is important to the institutions we surveyed.

Our survey suggests more rapid development of integration and/or interoperability between RIM systems and scholarly communications repositories in Europe than in the US and Canada, and, indeed, an **increasing overlap of practice, functionality, and workflows between previously siloed RIM systems and repository systems**. Further analysis needs to be carried out to tell to what extent these platforms are functionally enhanced RIM systems or rather "expanded repositories."

In addition, both functional integration and interoperability with RIM systems are weaker for data repositories than those for institutional repositories focused on publications. As the identification and curation of research datasets is a recent development, it is not surprising that practices are still developing, and this offers an interesting opportunity for follow up in future surveys.

Institutional Stakeholders and their Activities

The enterprise nature of RIM activity means that several institutional stakeholders may be involved and indeed responsible for different areas. In order to better understand this landscape, we asked respondents to name who, out of seven institutional stakeholders, has primary responsibility for each of fourteen RIM-related activities listed in the survey.

We found that in aggregate, the research office was reported as having responsibility for the greatest number of activities within the RIM enterprise, followed by the library, IT, and university academic leadership. This spread of responsibility and the level to which respondents selected that more than one office is *primarily* responsible reflects the campus-wide nature of RIM activity.

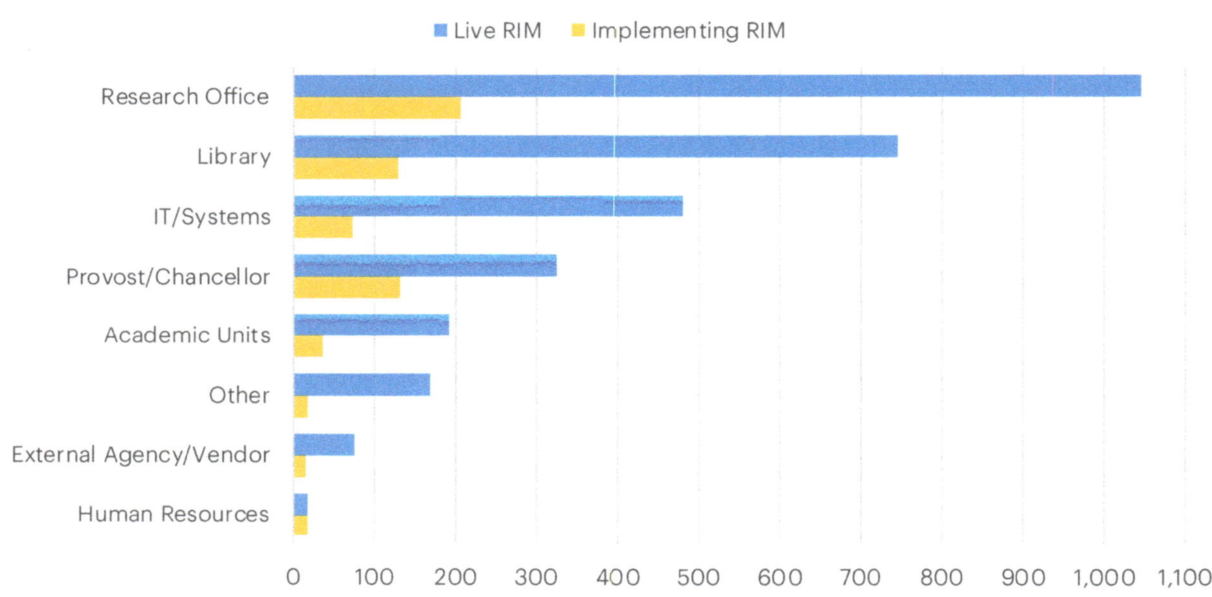

Stakeholders with "Primary Responsibility" for 14 Specific RIM Activities
by number of mentions
Live RIM
Implementing RIM
Research Office
Library
IT/Systems
Provost/Chancellor
Academic Units
Other
External Agency/Vendor
Human Resources
0
100
200
300
400
500
600
700
800
900
1,000
1,100

FIGURE 30. Primary stakeholders based on total number of mentions across all responses for all areas of activity, in aggregate. Note that multiple primary stakeholders could be selected per area of activity.

REGIONAL DIFFERENCES

It is clear that there are regional differences in the relative importance of different stakeholders. Figure 31 displays the relative importance of the library, research office, and other stakeholders, by country. The research office is more prominent than the library in most countries, particularly in Australia and the UK, which have well-established national assessment exercises. The Netherlands displays a somewhat unique profile, indicating that the library is a primary stakeholder and also demonstrating greater involvement from academic units rather than the research office.[43]

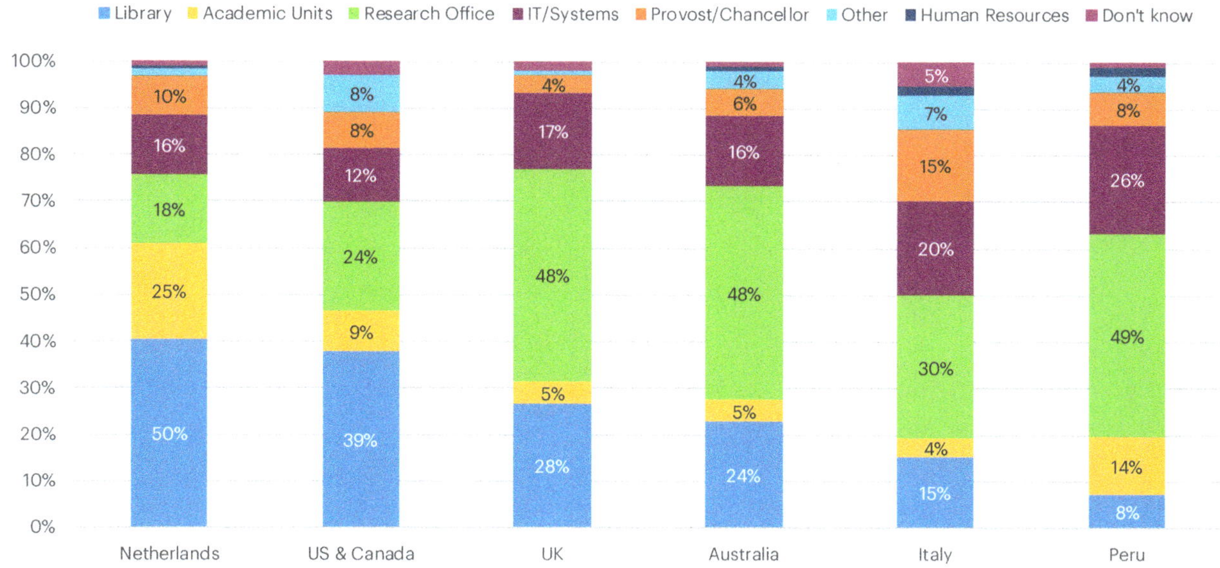
Stakeholders with Primary Responsibility for RIM Activities by Country
Library
Academic Units
Research Office
IT/Systems
Provost/Chancellor
Other
Human Resources
Don't know
100%
90%
80%
70%
60%
50%
40%
30%
20%
10%
0%
Netherlands
US & Canada
UK
Australia
Italy
Peru
50%
25%
18%
16%
10%
39%
9%
24%
12%
8%
8%
28%
5%
48%
17%
4%
24%
5%
48%
16%
6%
4%
15%
4%
30%
20%
15%
7%
5%
8%
14%
49%
26%
8%
4%

FIGURE 31. Relative importance of different stakeholders listed as "primary," organized by importance of the library, by selected countries and for all implementation stages.

Open-ended responses also emphasized the collaborative nature of RIM activity and the split of responsibilities on campus:

> "The responsibility of library departments concerns of open access repository building (repository is in preparation) and registration of institutional publication activity. Responsibility on CRIS system, Central /National Registry of Publication Activity and Central Registry of Theses and Dissertations has been delegated to the departments outside of library." **(Slovakia)**

> "Library administrates institutional repository and provides the link between the researcher information management system. In Japan especially national research universities hire University Research Administrators and they help RIM activities. But we could not hire enough number of URAs, so librarians and system engineers of the library are supporting Research Office, mainly providing the current information on trend on scholarly communication, metadata, IDs, and sometimes technology." **(Japan)**

> "Library has primary role in support[:] metadata entry, technical support, training, and workflow validation for the systems Publications module. Other modules of the system are primarily supported by our Information Technology." **(US)**

Some respondents emphasized that our effort to understand cross-divisional collaboration through structured survey questions sometimes did not adequately identify the cross-functional teams developing to support RIM at some institutions:

> "Librrians [sic] work in the support ad hoc office (together with IT experts and evaluation experts), but they are not in the library. Their work is independent from the library." **(Italy)**

And that libraries also sometimes had responsibility for processes more commonly seen in the research office:

> "The library is the Service Owner and Service Operating Manager for all university research information systems, including the pre award/post award system." **(UK)**

ROLE OF THE LIBRARY

In the literature, RIM is often seen from a purely administrative perspective with a focus on research administrators as primary stakeholders.[44] On the other hand, as a library organization, OCLC cannot fail to recognize the efforts many research libraries put into RIM activities and strategies, making RIM a potentially growing area of library engagement. In this survey, we were particularly interested to learn more about the roles of libraries in RIM.

Focusing on the library as primary stakeholder in any RIM activity, among institutions with a live RIM system, respondents reported that libraries most commonly played a leading role in activities such as open access, copyright, and deposit; metadata validation workflows; training and support; research data management; and metadata entry. These roles are congruent with established library expertise, drawing upon publications and scholarship expertise, and commitments to discoverability and access of research output, as well as reputational support.[45] Informants reported that libraries were least often primary stakeholders offering financial support, maintaining or servicing technical operations, and project management.

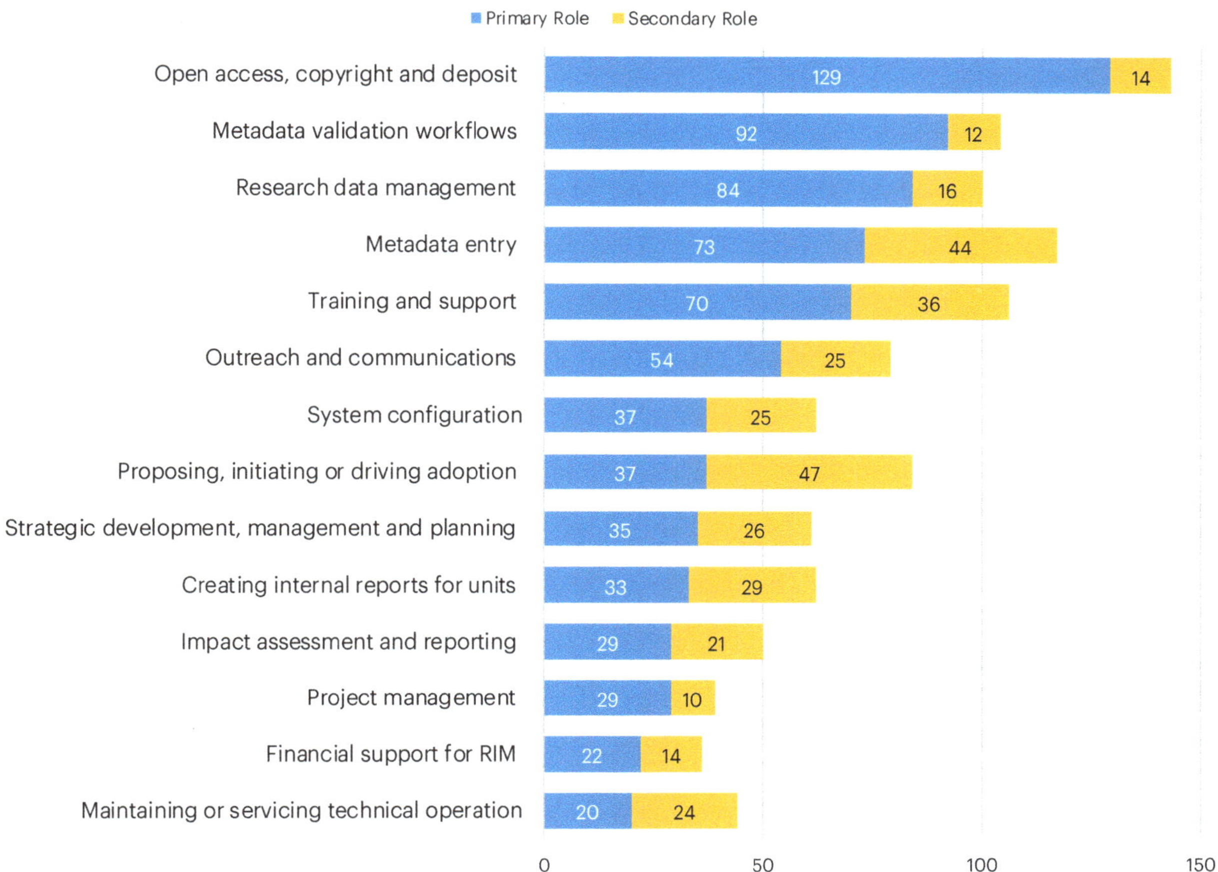
RIM Activities for which the Library Plays a Role (n=172)
Primary Role
Secondary Role
Open access, copyright and deposit
Metadata validation workflows
Research data management
Metadata entry
Training and support
Outreach and communications
System configuration
Proposing, initiating or driving adoption
Strategic development, management and planning
Creating internal reports for units
Impact assessment and reporting
Project management
Financial support for RIM
Maintaining or servicing technical operation
129
14
92
12
84
16
73
44
70
36
54
25
37
25
37
47
35
26
33
29
29
21
29
10
22
14
20
24
0
50
100
150

FIGURE 32. RIM activities for which the library plays a primary or supporting role, aggregated for institutions with a live RIM.

Figure 32 also displays aggregate responses for how libraries are playing a supporting, or secondary, role in some activities. In the context of this report, it is particularly notable that many institutions say that libraries play a supporting role in the proposing, initiating, or driving adoption of RIM. In fact, the proposing, initiating, or driving adoption of RIM is the most named role libraries play a supporting role in.

We were also interested to see if there were any regional differences in the importance of libraries as primary stakeholders by different RIM activity (figure 33). It is interesting to see that for countries with national assessment exercises, such as the UK, Australia, and Italy there is a marked reduction of the importance of libraries as primary stakeholders, compared to other countries with no national exercise, such as the United States. One explanation could be that where national assessment is in place, RIM systems are treated more as corporate systems with access to financial, technical, and project management support from other institutional stakeholders.

Open-ended responses illustrate the library's support of RIM activities such as open access through administration of the institutional repository; metadata entry and validation; and training and support. We also heard from respondents who noted the lack of (or wished for greater) library involvement:

"Library has primary role in support[:] metadata entry, technical support, training, and workflow validation for the systems Publications module." **(US)**

"Outputs harvested from Elements are displayed publicly via the institutional repository, and the Library make these outputs open access where possible." **(Australia)**

"Our library has chosen not to support any RIM activities at our institution." **(US)**

"I wish our library would take a more active role!" **(US)**

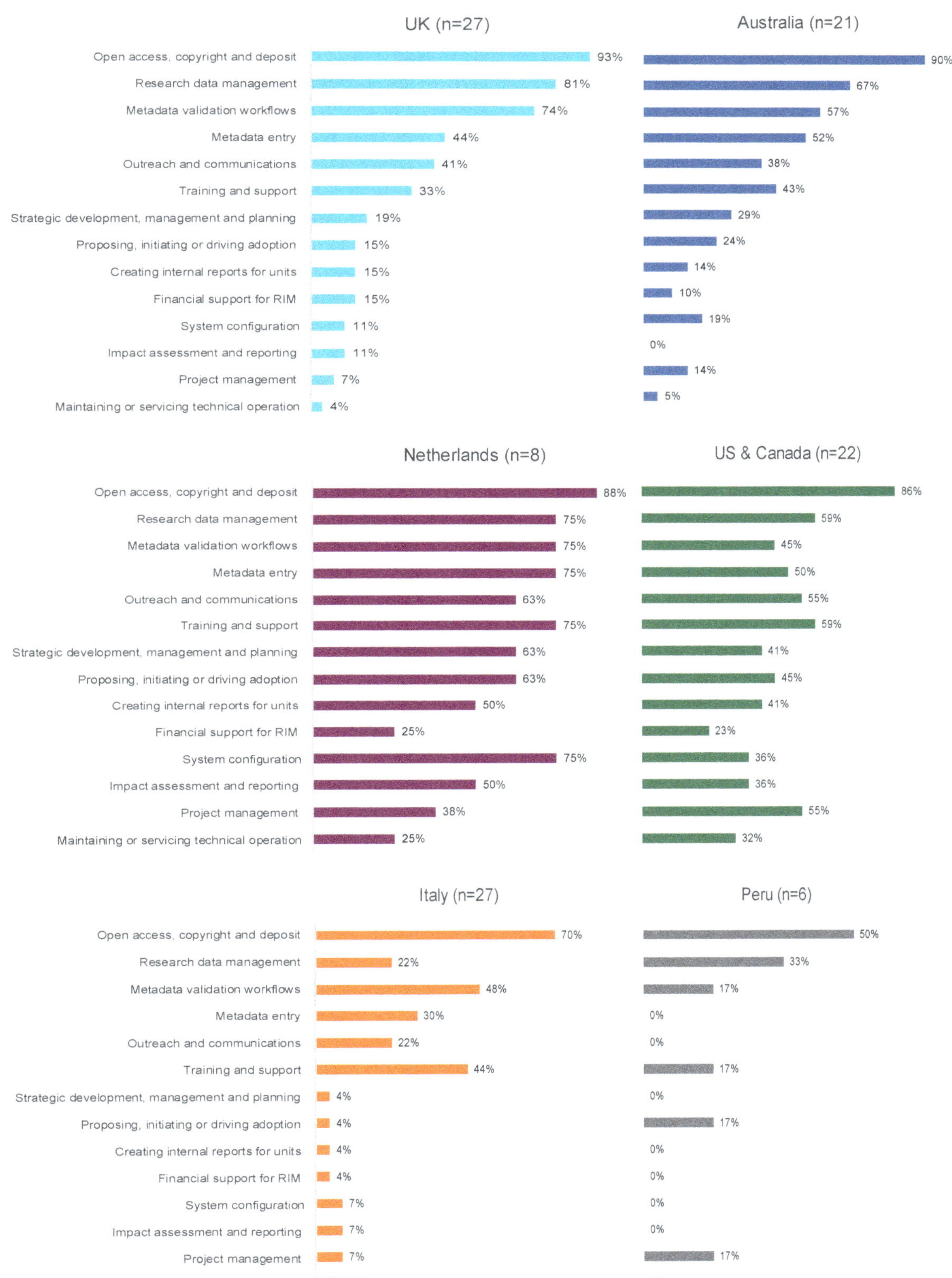
Library as Primary Stakeholder, by Country
UK (n=27)
Australia (n=21)
Netherlands (n=8)
US & Canada (n=22)
Italy (n=27)
Peru (n=6)
Open access, copyright and deposit
Research data management
Metadata validation workflows
Metadata entry
Outreach and communications
Training and support
Strategic development, management and planning
Proposing, initiating or driving adoption
Creating internal reports for units
Financial support for RIM
System configuration
Impact assessment and reporting
Project management
Maintaining or servicing technical operation
93% 81% 74% 44% 41% 33% 19% 15% 15% 15% 11% 11% 7% 4%
90% 67% 57% 52% 38% 43% 29% 24% 14% 10% 19% 0% 14% 5%
88% 75% 75% 75% 63% 75% 63% 63% 50% 25% 75% 50% 38% 25%
86% 59% 45% 50% 55% 59% 41% 45% 41% 23% 36% 36% 55% 32%
70% 22% 48% 30% 22% 44% 4% 4% 4% 4% 7% 7% 7% 7%
50% 33% 17% 0% 0% 17% 0% 17% 0% 0% 0% 0% 17% 0%

FIGURE 33. Percent of institutions at any stage of RIM engagement reporting the library as a primary stakeholder per activity.

We also asked respondents to identify the library unit(s) active in the implementation or support of RIM activities, and found that Research Services (59%) and Scholarly Communication (41%) units are the most likely to be active while, unsurprisingly, Teaching and Instruction units were the least likely.

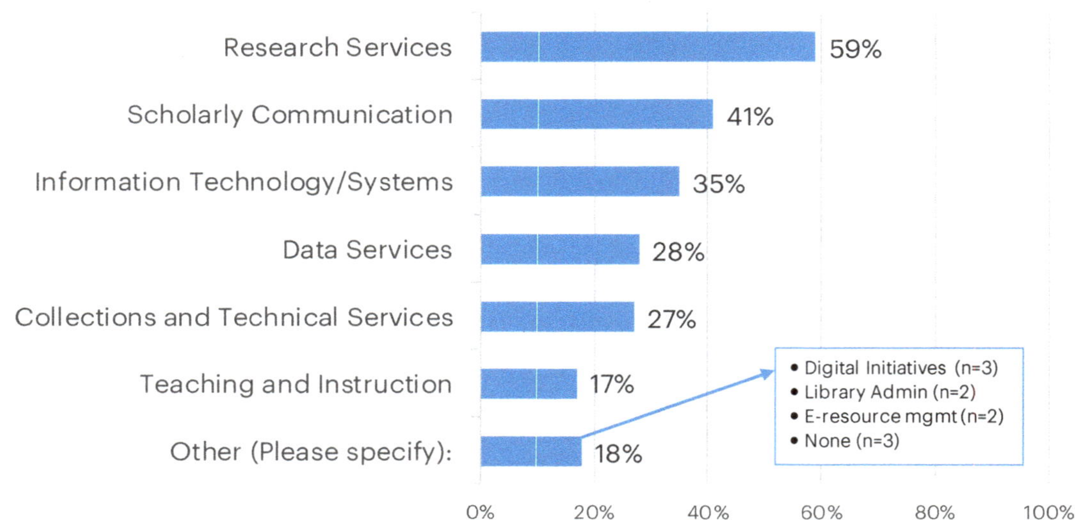
Library Units Supporting RIM Activities (n=150)
Note: Respondents could select more than one answer
Research Services
59%
Scholarly Communication
41%
Information Technology/Systems
35%
Data Services
28%
Collections and Technical Services
27%
Teaching and Instruction
17%
Other (Please specify):
18%
• Digital Initiatives (n=3)
• Library Admin (n=2)
• E-resource mgmt (n=2)
• None (n=3)
0%
20%
40%
60%
80%
100%

FIGURE 34. Library units supporting RIM activities at institutions with a live RIM system.

Libraries' principal goals in supporting RIM activities

Respondents were presented a list of 12 goals in supporting RIM activities and were asked to indicate the importance of each goal for their library.

Not surprisingly, nearly half of respondents (47%) with a live RIM system indicate that stewardship of the institution's scholarly output, aid to scholars complying with open data requirements, and support for open access to scholarly literature are extremely important goals for the library. Furthermore, more than half (53%) of responding institutions described support for institutional strategic objectives as an extremely important goal for the library.

The least important goals relate to the collection and facilitation of bibliometrics data for both the tracking of campus scholarship and the support of promotion and tenure activities.

...more than half (53%) of responding institutions described support for institutional strategic objectives as an extremely important goal for the library.

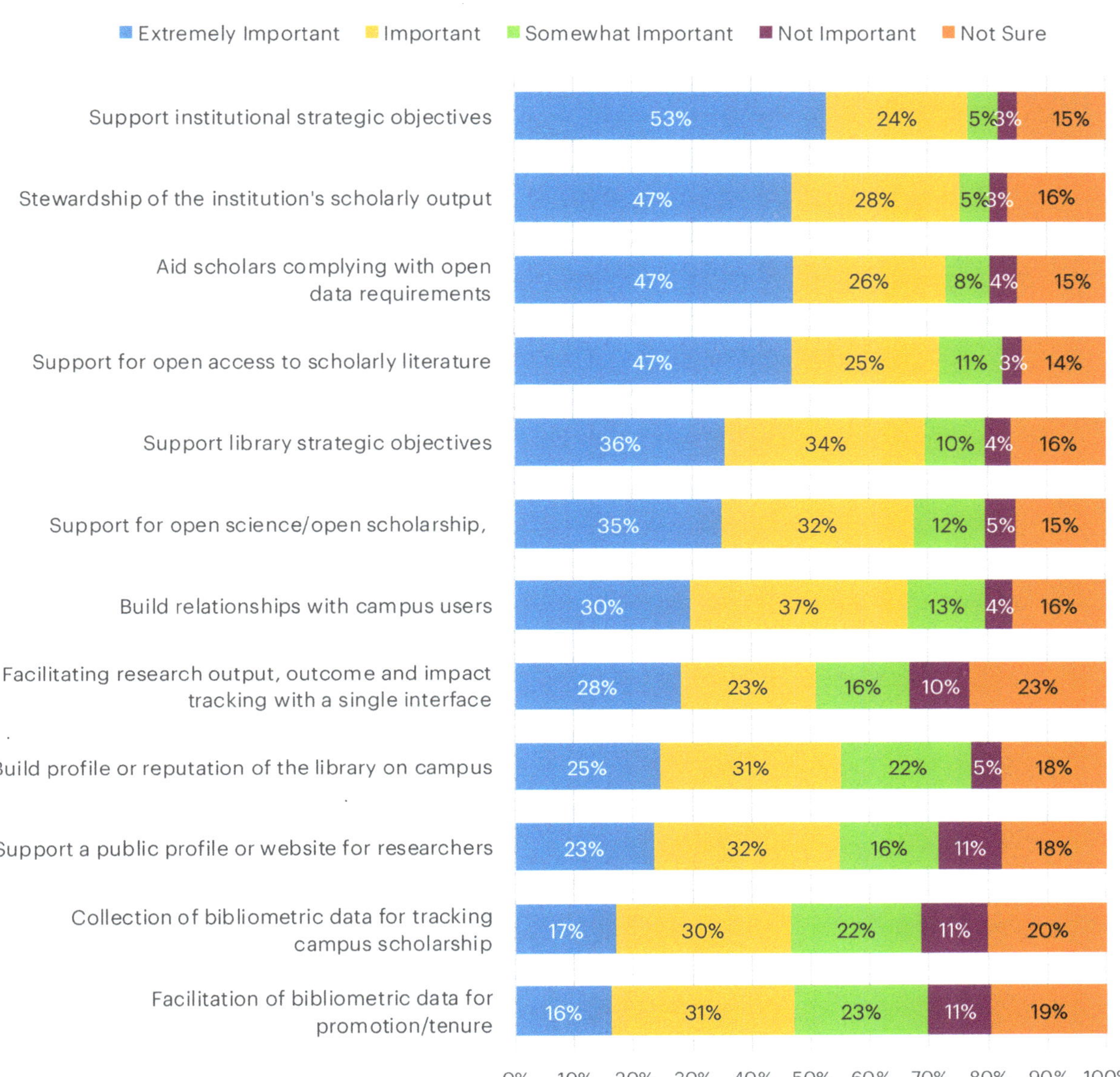
Important Library Goals in Supporting RIM Activities (n=159)
Extremely Important
Important
Somewhat Important
Not Important
Not Sure
Support institutional strategic objectives
53%
24%
5%
3%
15%
Stewardship of the institution's scholarly output
47%
28%
5%
3%
16%
Aid scholars complying with open data requirements
47%
26%
8%
4%
15%
Support for open access to scholarly literature
47%
25%
11%
3%
14%
Support library strategic objectives
36%
34%
10%
4%
16%
Support for open science/open scholarship,
35%
32%
12%
5%
15%
Build relationships with campus users
30%
37%
13%
4%
16%
Facilitating research output, outcome and impact tracking with a single interface
28%
23%
16%
10%
23%
Build profile or reputation of the library on campus
25%
31%
22%
5%
18%
Support a public profile or website for researchers
23%
32%
16%
11%
18%
Collection of bibliometric data for tracking campus scholarship
17%
30%
22%
11%
20%
Facilitation of bibliometric data for promotion/tenure
16%
31%
23%
11%
19%
0%
10%
20%
30%
40%
50%
60%
70%
80%
90%
100%

FIGURE 35. Important library goals in supporting RIM activities, at institutions with a live RIM system.

When we subdivide this data by selected countries, we can observe some regional differences. It is clear that Australia, the Netherlands, and the UK consider many of the goals listed as extremely important or important for libraries—countries in which national and funder open science policies are prominent. But the responses from US and Italian institutions, and the small sample from Germany, suggest that they define the library's role very differently, focusing on a smaller subset of RIM activities and potentially even not considering RIM activities as key library goals at all. This is generally congruent with weaker national open science mandates, but could additionally be rooted in a lack of available human resources to take on the work, especially in institutions where RIM workflows have not yet had the time to mature. RIM work can be quite demanding and resource-intensive, as will be discussed in the next chapter.

Library Goals for Supporting RIM Activities, for Selected Countries

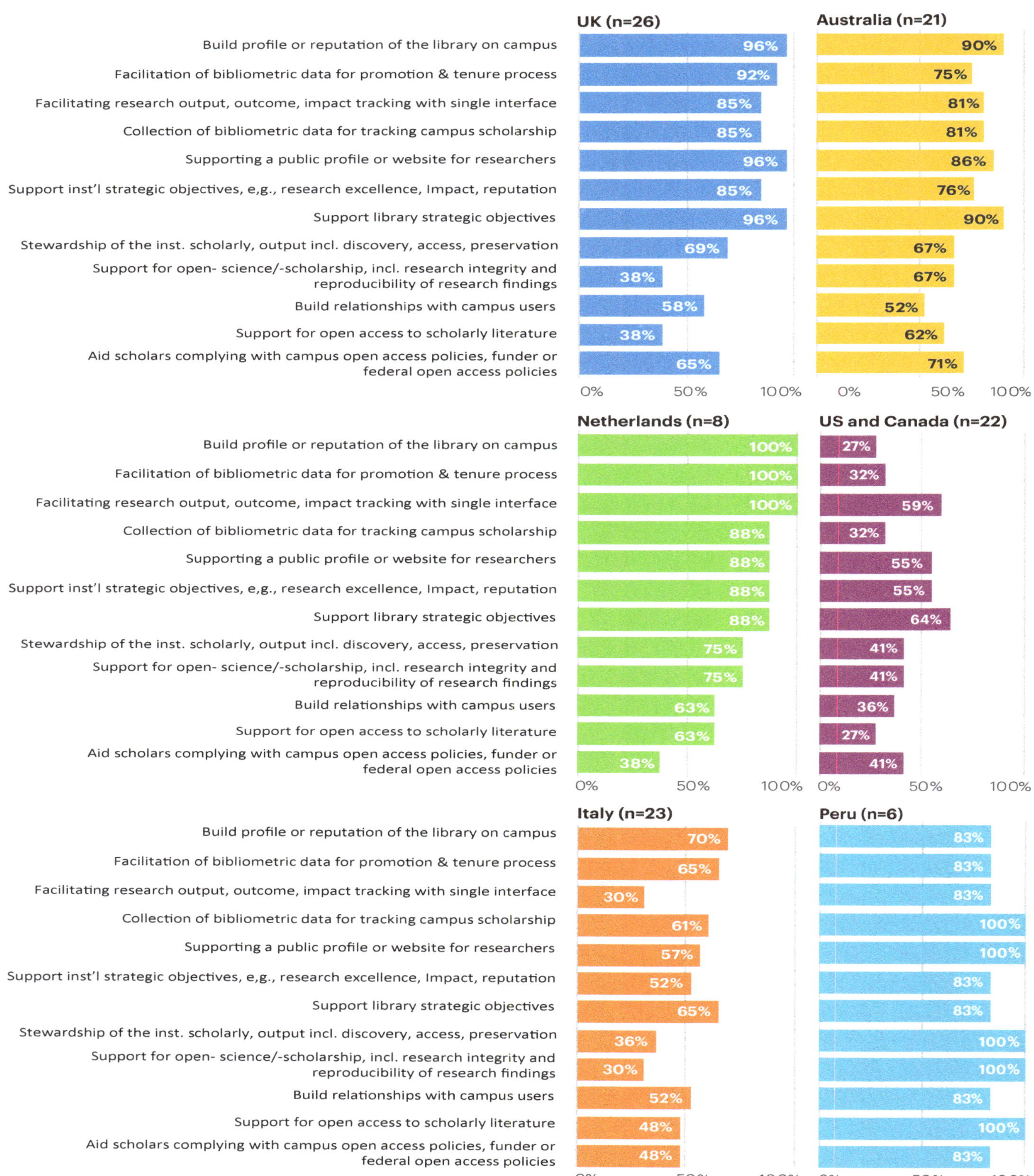

UK (n=26)
Australia (n=21)
Netherlands (n=8)
US and Canada (n=22)
Italy (n=23)
Peru (n=6)
Build profile or reputation of the library on campus
Facilitation of bibliometric data for promotion & tenure process
Facilitating research output, outcome, impact tracking with single interface
Collection of bibliometric data for tracking campus scholarship
Supporting a public profile or website for researchers
Support inst'l strategic objectives, e,g., research excellence, Impact, reputation
Support library strategic objectives
Stewardship of the inst. scholarly, output incl. discovery, access, preservation
Support for open- science/-scholarship, incl. research integrity and reproducibility of research findings
Build relationships with campus users
Support for open access to scholarly literature
Aid scholars complying with campus open access policies, funder or federal open access policies
UK: 96%, 92%, 85%, 85%, 96%, 85%, 96%, 69%, 38%, 58%, 38%, 65%
Australia: 90%, 75%, 81%, 81%, 86%, 76%, 90%, 67%, 67%, 52%, 62%, 71%
Netherlands: 100%, 100%, 100%, 88%, 88%, 88%, 88%, 75%, 75%, 63%, 63%, 38%
US and Canada: 27%, 32%, 59%, 32%, 55%, 55%, 64%, 41%, 41%, 36%, 27%, 41%
Italy: 70%, 65%, 30%, 61%, 57%, 52%, 65%, 36%, 30%, 52%, 48%, 48%
Peru: 83%, 83%, 83%, 100%, 100%, 83%, 83%, 100%, 100%, 83%, 100%, 83%
0%
50%
100%

FIGURE 36. Extremely important and important library goals in supporting RIM activities for institutions with live RIM system, for selected countries.

HUMAN RESOURCES SUPPORT

Considerable staff resources are dedicated to supporting RIM activities at many institutions, and in this survey we sought to better understand resource allocations for both library and non-library units.

Due to the way the questions were formulated, we cannot identify exact numbers of staff or FTE involved; however, we can offer some observations on the minimum numbers of FTE and separate members of staff involved—full time or part time, library or otherwise.

A fifth (21%) of respondents indicate their library has three or more staff supporting RIM activities full time; and just over a quarter (27%) have one or two FTE library staff involved.

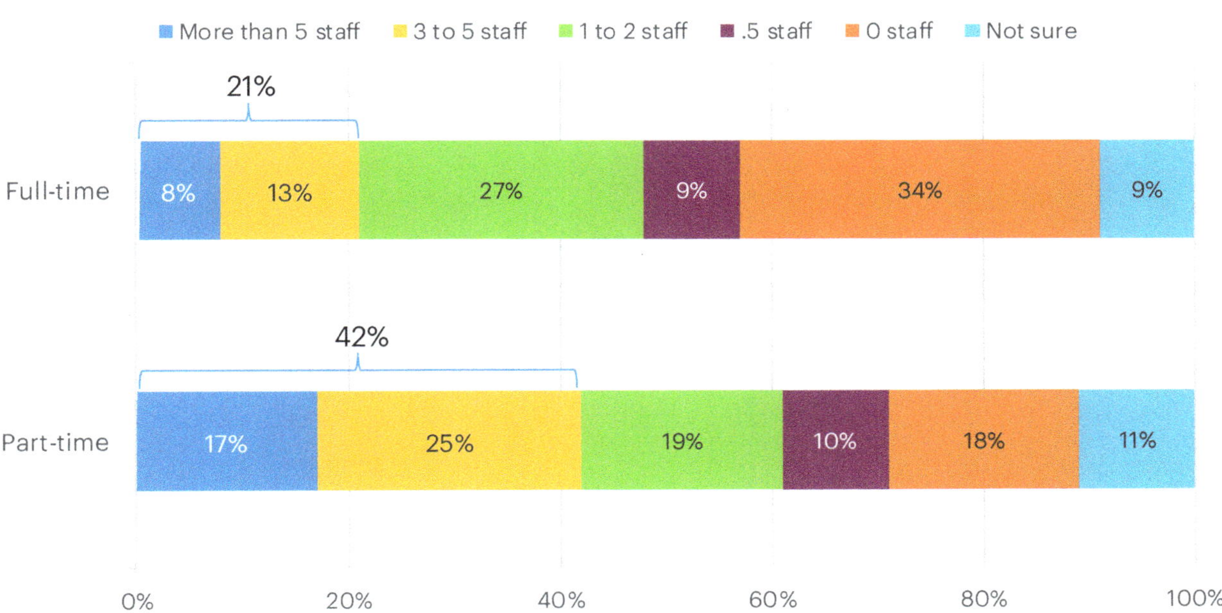

Number of Library Staff Supporting RIM Activities (n=159)
More than 5 staff
3 to 5 staff
1 to 2 staff
.5 staff
0 staff
Not sure
21%
Full-time
8%
13%
27%
9%
34%
9%
42%
Part-time
17%
25%
19%
10%
18%
11%
0%
20%
40%
60%
80%
100%

FIGURE 37. Number of library staff supporting RIM activities full- or part-time, for institutions with a live RIM system.

For non-library staff, numbers are even higher—a third (30%) of respondents indicate their institution has three or more non-library staff supporting RIM activities full time, and slightly less (27%) have one or two FTE non-library full-time staff supporting RIM.

About 30% of respondents indicate not having any full-time library staff working on RIM; similarly, 30% of respondents indicate not having any full-time non-library staff supporting RIM. This accounts for the comparatively high number of "zero" responses in figure 38. Where no full-time staff was involved, part-time staff was. No institution reported zero aggregate institutional staff support for their RIM activities. In verbatim comments, some respondents emphasized the importance of adequate staffing:

"A RIM service gives institutions the opportunity to examine the entirety of their research endeavours, to determine strengths and weaknesses, and look for opportunities. It is however important to realize that the acquisition of the system on its own will not solve any issues the institution may be encountering - an adequate number of trained staff is vtal [sic] to ensure that the system is utilized to its fullest extent." **(UK)**

"The levels resources (person, time, financial) needed to effectively implement and support RIMs can be higher than initial estimates, regardless of the platform." **(US)**

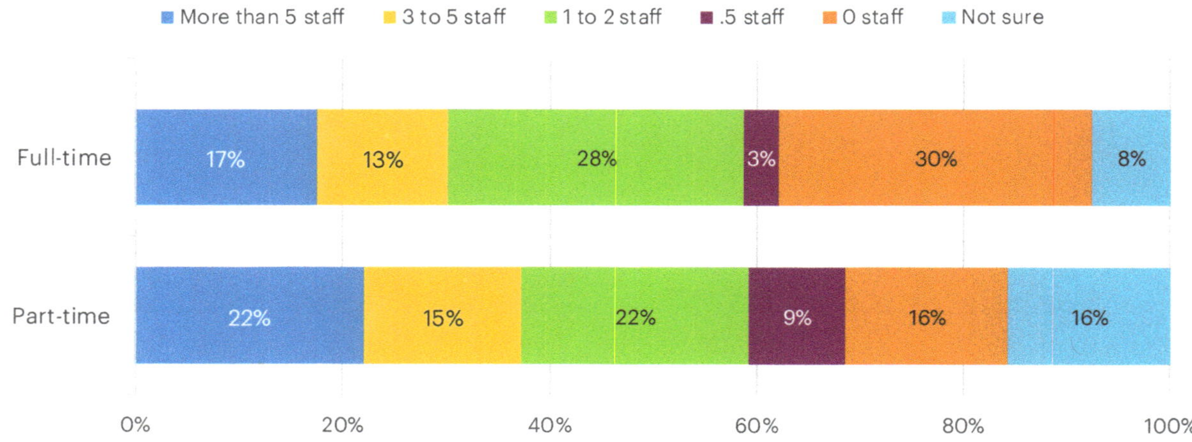
Number of Institution Staff Supporting RIM Activities (n=172)
More than 5 staff
3 to 5 staff
1 to 2 staff
.5 staff
0 staff
Not sure
Full-time
17%
13%
28%
3%
30%
8%
Part-time
22%
15%
22%
9%
16%
16%
0%
20%
40%
60%
80%
100%

FIGURE 38. Number of non-library staff supporting RIM activities full- or part-time, for institutions with a live RIM system.

TABLE 1. For institutions with live RIM systems, the number of institutions reporting staffing in various library- and non-library staffing ranges.

Number of FTE	Library Full-time	Library part-time	Non-library full-time	Non-library part-time
0	54	28	52	27
0.5	14	16	6	16
1-2	43	31	49	38
3-5	21	39	22	26
More than 5	12	27	30	38
Not sure	15	18	13	27

Overall, when aggregating library and non-library staff numbers, about two-thirds of the institutions report having at least two full-time staff members supporting RIM activities. Some institutions dedicate more resources to this effort: a third of institutions report at least five full-time staff members supporting RIM, and eight institutions reported RIM staff support in excess of ten FTE.

RIM clearly is a true team effort, and, in most cases, also a cross-divisional one, combining human resources from diverse institutional units.

Looking at full-time and part-time staff combined from both the library and other units, two thirds of the respondents report having at least five, one third at least ten members of staff working on RIM full time or part time.

RIM clearly is a true team effort, and, in most cases, also a cross-divisional one, combining human resources from diverse institutional units. Only very few institutions indicated that only library staff (eight of 159) are involved with RIM, or only non-library staff (eight of 172).

INSTITUTIONAL POPULATIONS INCLUDED IN RIM

As we prepared this survey, we recognized institutional and regional differences in the disciplinary and campus populations included in local RIM systems. Respondents were presented a list of seven types of populations on campus and were asked to indicate which have records in the RIM system.

Institutions nearly universally (95%) reported the inclusion of academics, researchers, lecturers, scholars, and faculty members in the RIM system.

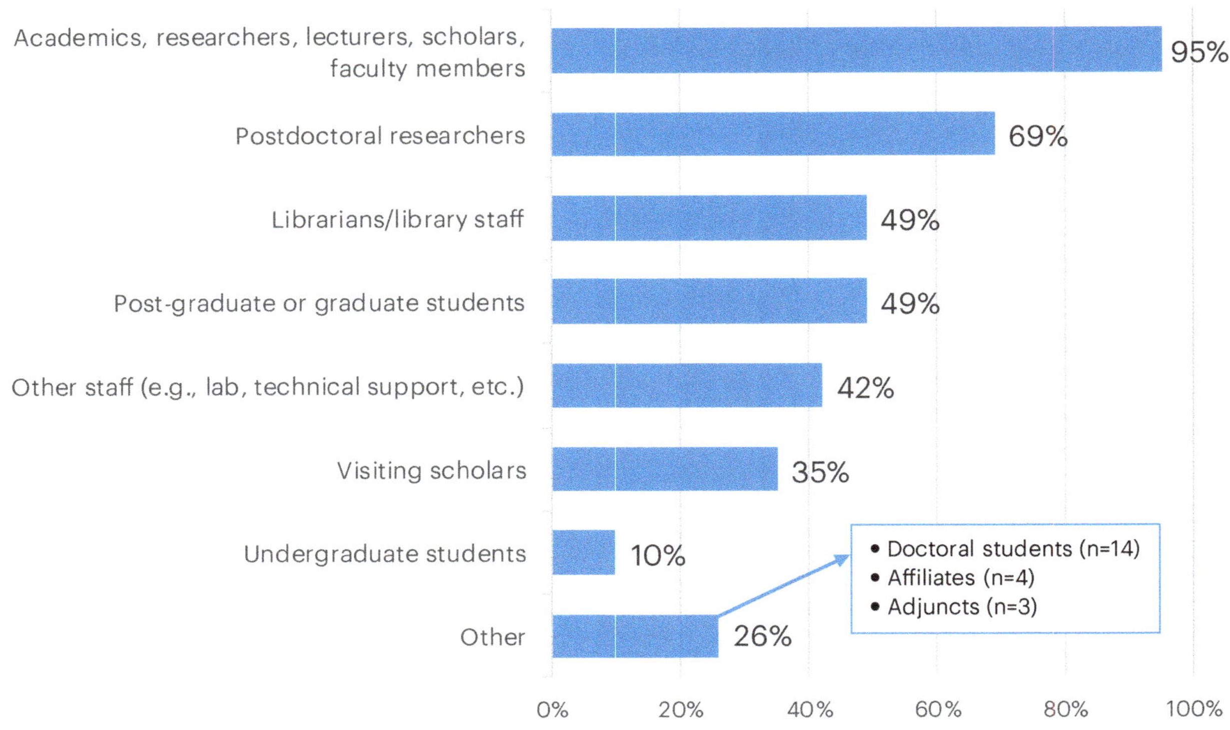
Campus Populations with Records in RIM System (n=166)
Note: Respondents could select more than one answer
Academics, researchers, lecturers, scholars, faculty members
95%
Postdoctoral researchers
69%
Librarians/library staff
49%
Post-graduate or graduate students
49%
Other staff (e.g., lab, technical support, etc.)
42%
Visiting scholars
35%
Undergraduate students
10%
Other
26%
• Doctoral students (n=14)
• Affiliates (n=4)
• Adjuncts (n=3)
0%
20%
40%
60%
80%
100%

FIGURE 39. Campus populations with records in the live RIM system.

The distinctions occur when other populations are considered. For instance, 69% of respondents report including postdoctoral researchers in their RIM and half indicate librarians/library staff and post-graduate/graduate students (49%, each) have records in the RIM system. That number likely increases when observing that fourteen institutions also specified that doctoral students (a more precise term than the "post-graduate or graduate students" category offered in the survey) are included in their RIM. Over a third have other staff, such as lab or technical support (42%), or visiting scholars (35%) included, while a tenth (10%) indicate undergraduate students have records in the RIM system.

Examined regionally, the inclusion of postdoctoral researchers is widespread in some locales (90% among Australian institutions and 80% across European institutions), but less common in others (only 36% among US and Canadian institutions). The differences are less striking but similar for post-graduate students.

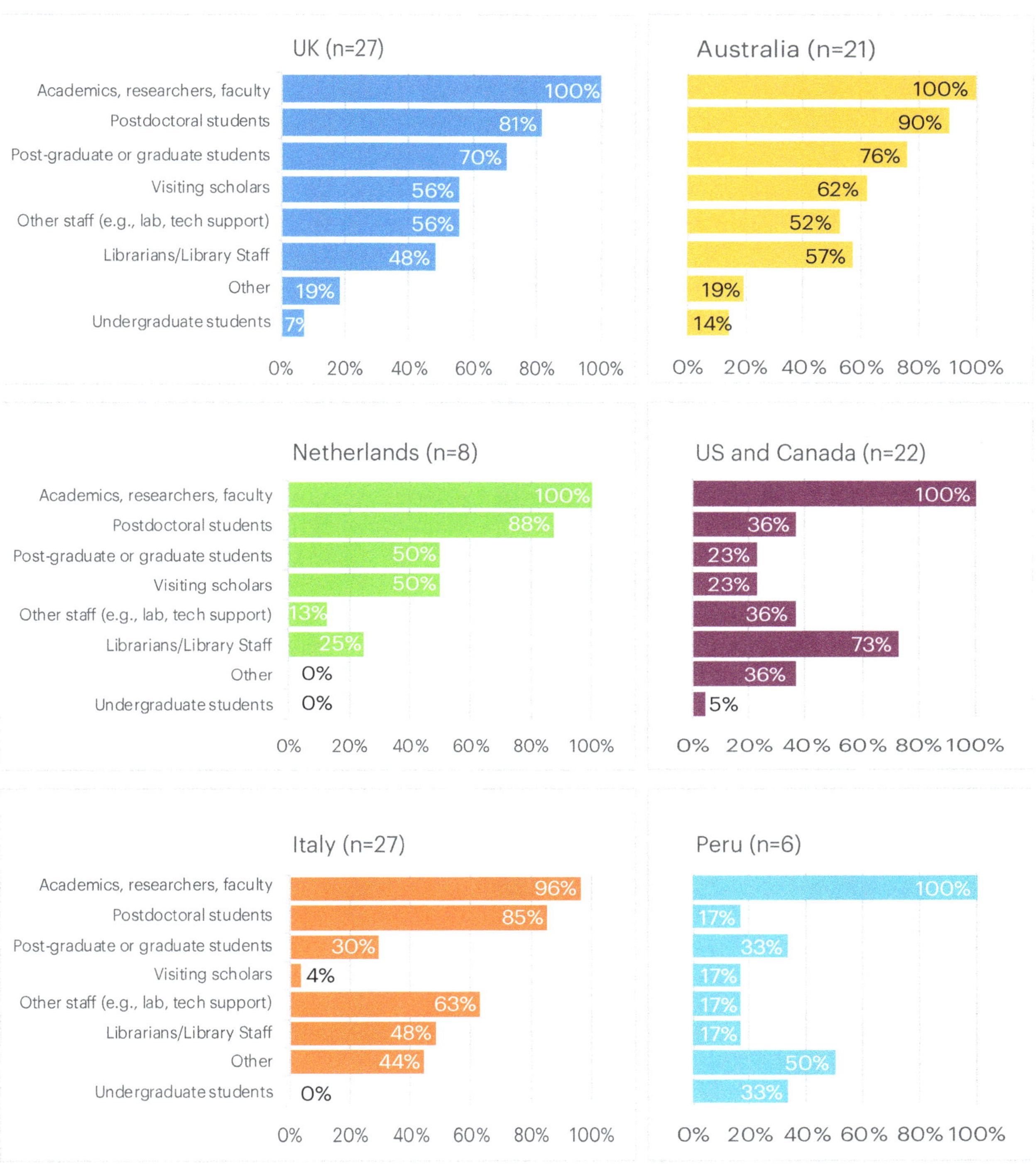

Institutional Populations Represented in RIM Systems, for Selected Countries
UK (n=27)
Australia (n=21)
Netherlands (n=8)
US and Canada (n=22)
Italy (n=27)
Peru (n=6)
Academics, researchers, faculty
Postdoctoral students
Post-graduate or graduate students
Visiting scholars
Other staff (e.g., lab, tech support)
Librarians/Library Staff
Other
Undergraduate students
100%
81%
70%
56%
56%
48%
19%
7%
100%
90%
76%
62%
52%
57%
19%
14%
100%
88%
50%
50%
13%
25%
0%
0%
100%
36%
23%
23%
36%
73%
36%
5%
96%
85%
30%
4%
63%
48%
44%
0%
100%
17%
33%
17%
17%
17%
50%
33%
0% 20% 40% 60% 80% 100%

FIGURE 40. Populations with profiles in the RIM system, for institutions with live RIM systems, by region.

OUTREACH AND ASSESSMENT

We asked respondents to tell us if and how they were working to support RIM adoption at their institutions.

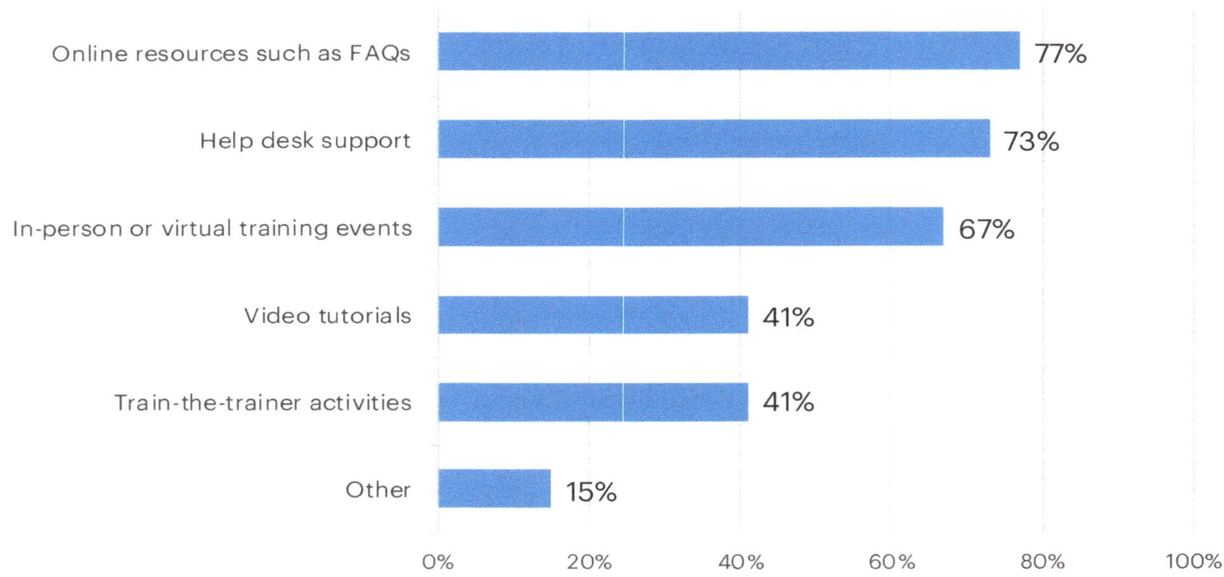

Activities Used to Support RIM Adoption (n=158)
Note: Respondents could select more than one answer
Online resources such as FAQs
77%
Help desk support
73%
In-person or virtual training events
67%
Video tutorials
41%
Train-the-trainer activities
41%
Other
15%
0%
20%
40%
60%
80%
100%

FIGURE 41. Institutional activities to support RIM adoption at institutions with a live RIM system.

The majority of institutions reported one or more activities to provide support and training to institutional users of RIM systems. Our question did not distinguish between training of staff members and researchers, who might also be expected to interact with the RIM system through their own user interface. Over three quarters of institutions with a live RIM system report offering online resources such as a list of frequently asked questions to support users interacting with the RIM. Nearly as many indicated they offered help desk support. Many also offered in-person, virtual training, video tutorials, or train-the-trainer activities.

We also asked institutions if and how they were collecting metrics to assess RIM usage.

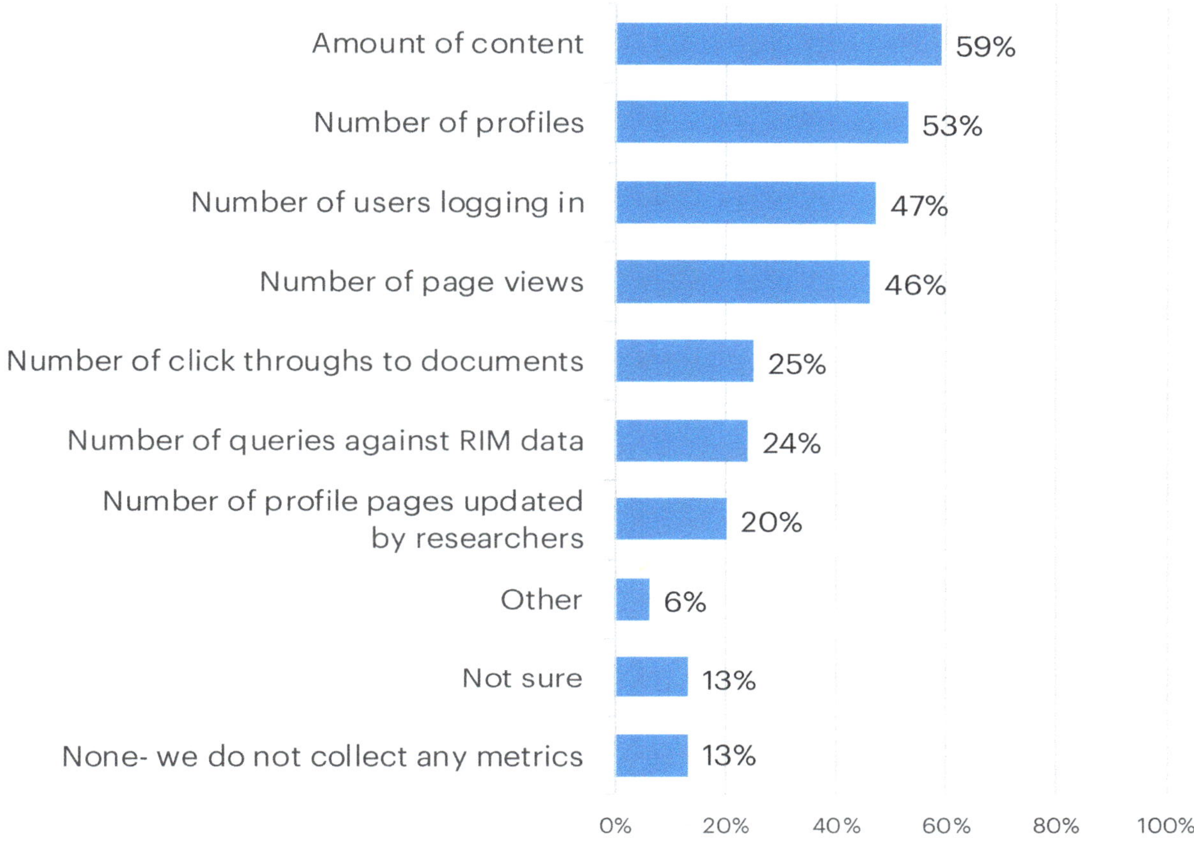
RIM Use Metrics Collected (n=143)
Note: Respondents could select more than one answer
Amount of content
59%
Number of profiles
53%
Number of users logging in
47%
Number of page views
46%
Number of click throughs to documents
25%
Number of queries against RIM data
24%
Number of profile pages updated by researchers
20%
Other
6%
Not sure
13%
None- we do not collect any metrics
13%
0%
20%
40%
60%
80%
100%

FIGURE 42. RIM metrics collected by institutions with a live RIM system.

Among responding institutions with a live RIM, we found that a slight majority of institutions reported collecting metrics concerning the overall amount of content in the RIM (59%) and the number of researcher profiles (53%). While some institutions reported other types of metrics, such as click-throughs to full-text documents or the number of page views, none of these exceeded 50%.

Finally, we also asked institutions about their efforts to measure the impact of the research information management activities, on elements such as time or cost savings or the ability of the institution to track scholarly activity.

In all categories offered, fewer than 40% of respondents with a live RIM system indicated that their institution was currently measuring the impact of their RIM. Overall, fewer than 10% of respondents indicated that their institution was tracking staff time savings or cost savings, although over 35% report that they would like to.

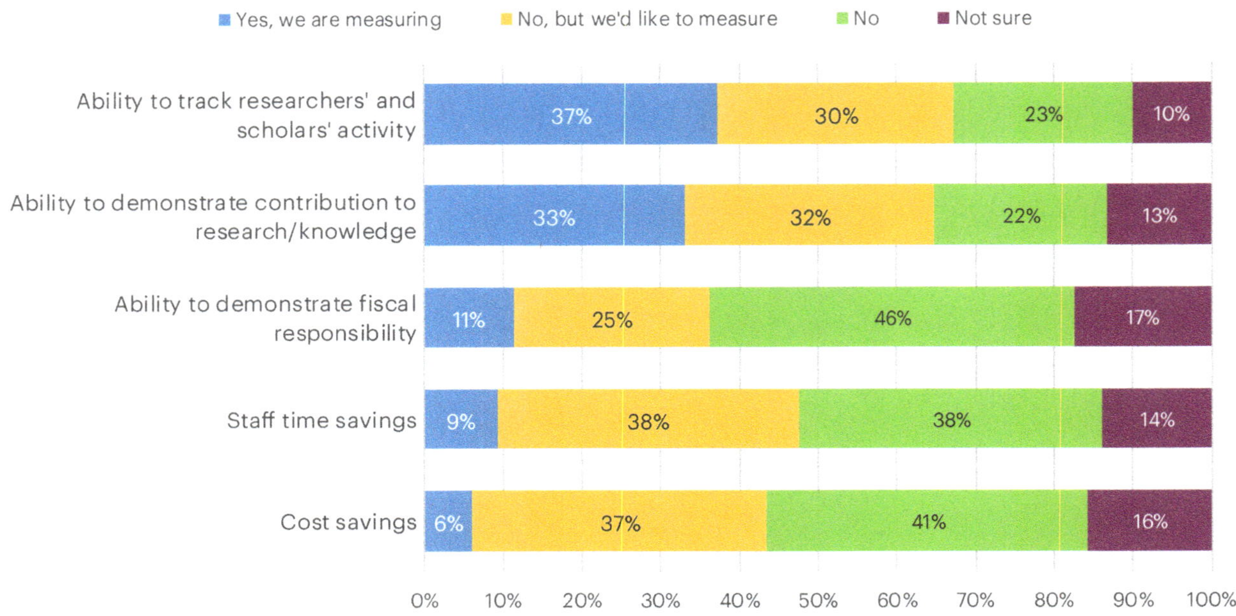
To What Extent Are You Measuring the Impact of RIM Use On...
Yes, we are measuring
No, but we'd like to measure
No
Not sure
Ability to track researchers' and scholars' activity
37%
30%
23%
10%
Ability to demonstrate contribution to research/knowledge
33%
32%
22%
13%
Ability to demonstrate fiscal responsibility
11%
25%
46%
17%
Staff time savings
9%
38%
38%
14%
Cost savings
6%
37%
41%
16%
0%
10%
20%
30%
40%
50%
60%
70%
80%
90%
100%

FIGURE 43. Institutional efforts to measure RIM impact at institutions with live RIM implementations.

SUMMARY: INSTITUTIONAL STAKEHOLDERS AND THEIR ACTIVITIES

> "It is well tailored to the specific requirements in terms of external stakeholder requirements. Furthermore, having the CRIS at the centre of the workflows enables an effective collaboration across different institutional units." **(UK)**

RIM systems were primarily used at the beginning as administrative tools for the research office, but now it seems their role and perception is evolving.

We found that, in aggregate, the research office has responsibility for the greatest number of activities within the RIM enterprise, with the library as a strong second most important player. **Responsibility for RIM activities is spread campus-wide and often shared between more than one office.** The cross-stakeholder nature of RIM activity can be seen as a potential facilitator in raising the profile of the library at the institution and vice-versa.

Libraries most commonly played a leading role in activities such as open access, copyright and deposit; metadata validation workflows; training and support; research data management; and metadata entry. Open-ended responses further emphasized that these library interactions were often related to the library's responsibility for one or more scholarly communications repositories. **More than half of responding institutions described support for institutional strategic objectives as extremely important for the library.**

This is congruent with the model previously developed in a position paper on RIM and the library's role in it, where the authors describe four critical ways in which libraries can support institutional research information management:[46]

Libraries in Research Information Management

Publications & Scholarship Expertise

Training & Support

Discoverability, Access & Reputational Support

Stewardship of the Institutional Record

FIGURE 44. Key roles for libraries in research information management from *Research Information Management: Defining RIM and the Library's Role* (doi.org/10.25333/C3NK88), CC BY 4.0.

Regarding the efforts involved in making this kind of support happen, respondents to our survey indicated that **they dedicate considerable human resources to support RIM activities, and usually in a cross-divisional effort.** Although a wide range of staffing levels were reported, in general, institutions tend to have more non-library than library staff supporting RIM activities: about two-thirds of the institutions report having at least two full-time staff members supporting RIM activities.

Institutions nearly universally (95%) reported the inclusion of academics, researchers, lecturers, scholars, and faculty members in the RIM system, and we note that, regionally, the inclusion of postdoctoral researchers and graduate students is more common in Australia and Europe than elsewhere. **Institutions widely reported the development of resources like online FAQs and help-desk support to encourage local RIM adoption**, but few institutions report current efforts to measure the impact or return on investment of their RIM system.

Interoperability

RIM, by definition, is part of a wider ecosystem of connections and dependencies. At the institution level and beyond, information is pulled in and pushed out, synchronized and harmonized, analyzed and reported on in different formats for different audiences and purposes.

The previous section explored RIM as an activity involving many institutional stakeholders with different roles and responsibilities. This section will focus on interoperability at the systems and data level.

INTERNAL AND EXTERNAL SYSTEMS

Respondents were asked with which internal and external systems their current RIM system interoperates.

For internal system interoperability, the majority of respondents with live RIM systems indicate their RIM system interoperates with institutional human resources systems (78%) and authentication systems (76%). For implementing institutions (n=42), this is similar with slightly lower percentages (62% and 52%).

Interoperability levels with repositories are significantly lower in comparison, in part due to the increasing merging of RIM and IR functional categories.

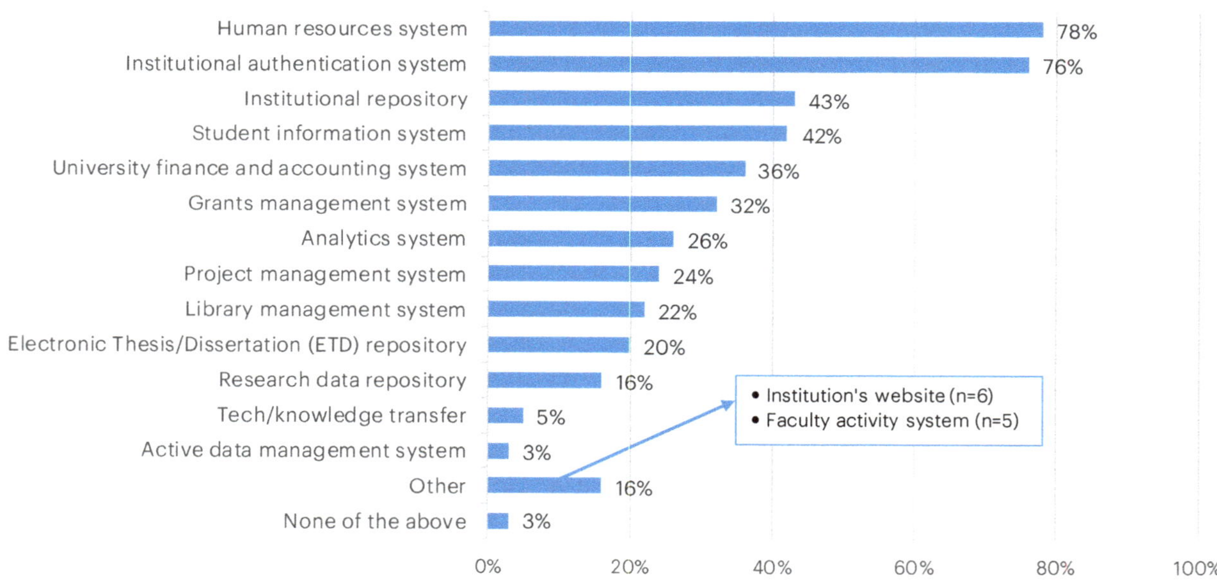
Internal Systems that Interoperate with Your RIM System (n=184)
Note: Respondents could select more than one answer
Human resources system
78%
Institutional authentication system
76%
Institutional repository
43%
Student information system
42%
University finance and accounting system
36%
Grants management system
32%
Analytics system
26%
Project management system
24%
Library management system
22%
Electronic Thesis/Dissertation (ETD) repository
20%
Research data repository
16%
Tech/knowledge transfer
5%
Active data management system
3%
Other
16%
None of the above
3%
• Institution's website (n=6)
• Faculty activity system (n=5)
0%
20%
40%
60%
80%
100%

FIGURE 45. Internal systems with which live RIM systems interoperate.

For external systems, the majority of respondents indicate their RIM interoperates with publication metadata sources and researcher/author ID registries among both live (76% and 65%, respectively) and implementing (64% and 57%) institutions, thus highlighting the importance of metadata harvesting for current and future implementations of RIM, as analyzed further in the next section.

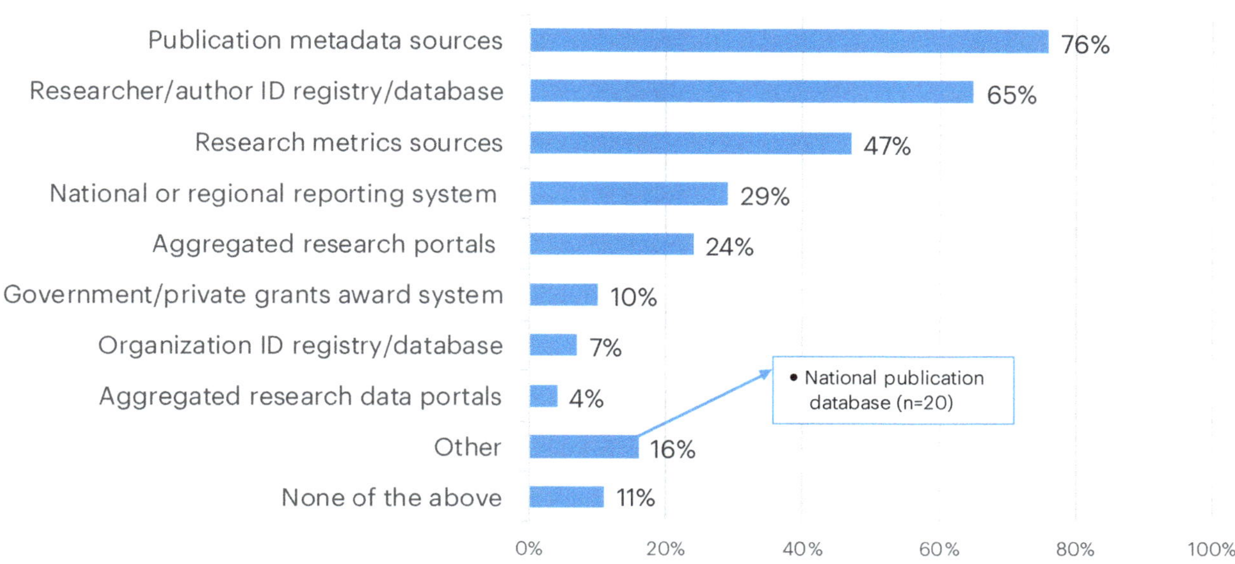
External Systems that Interoperate with Your RIM System (n=178)
Note: Respondents could select more than one answer
Publication metadata sources
76%
Researcher/author ID registry/database
65%
Research metrics sources
47%
National or regional reporting system
29%
Aggregated research portals
24%
Government/private grants award system
10%
Organization ID registry/database
7%
Aggregated research data portals
4%
Other
16%
None of the above
11%
• National publication database (n=20)
0%
20%
40%
60%
80%
100%

FIGURE 46. External systems live RIM systems interoperate with.

METADATA SOURCES POPULATING RIM SYSTEMS

Respondents were presented with fifteen sources of publication metadata and were asked to indicate which are used to populate their live RIM systems.

The majority of respondents indicated their RIM system is populated by Scopus (72%), Web of Science (63%), and PubMed (61%), followed by Crossref, ArXiv, and Europe PubMed Central. Notably, there is a long tail of additional metadata sources, including Google Books, that institutions are making use of to populate their RIM with suitable publications metadata.

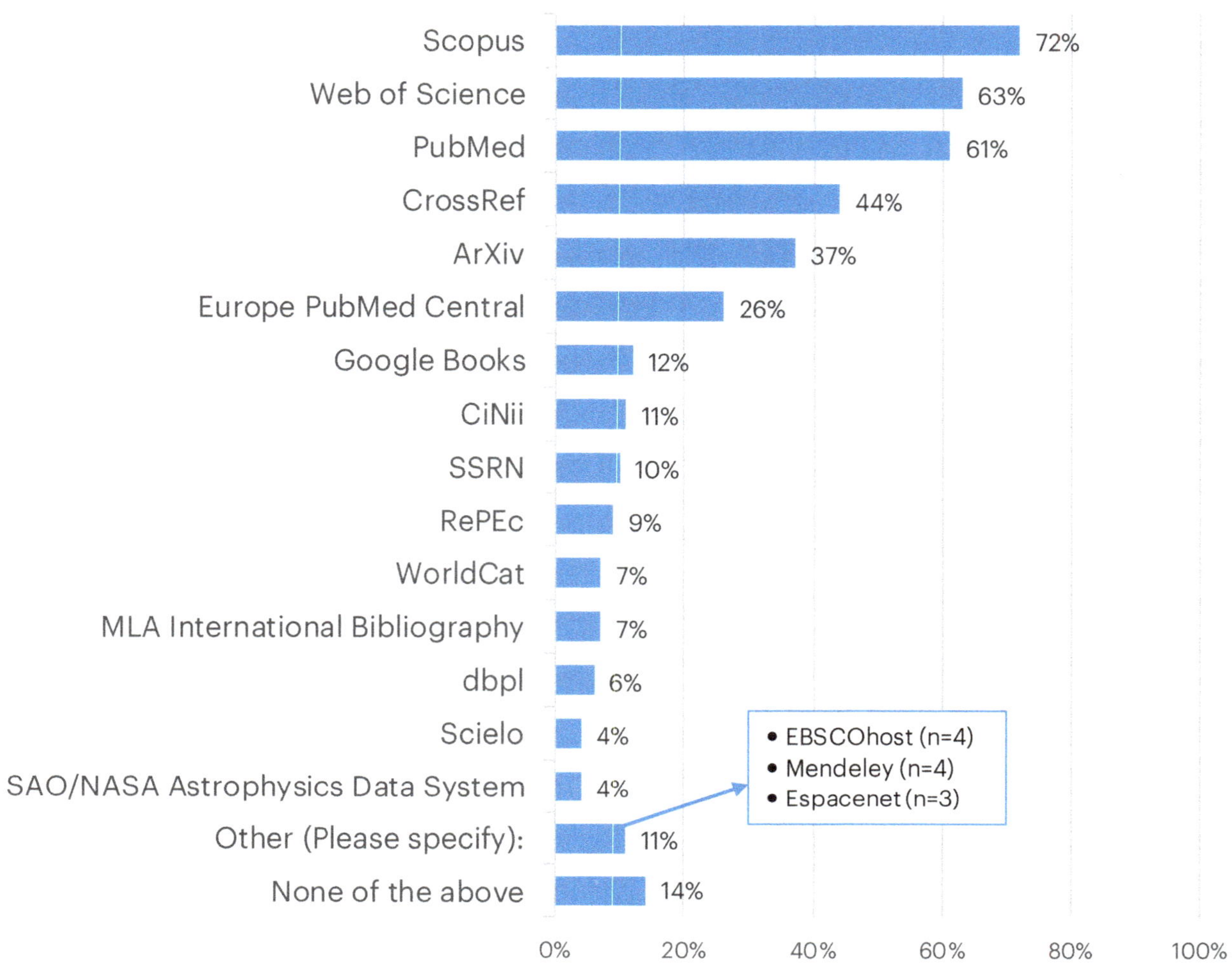
Publication Metadata Sources that Populate Your RIM System (n=185)
Note: Respondents could select more than one answer
Scopus
Web of Science
PubMed
CrossRef
ArXiv
Europe PubMed Central
Google Books
CiNii
SSRN
RePEc
WorldCat
MLA International Bibliography
dbpl
Scielo
SAO/NASA Astrophysics Data System
Other (Please specify):
None of the above
72%
63%
61%
44%
37%
26%
12%
11%
10%
9%
7%
7%
6%
4%
4%
11%
14%
• EBSCOhost (n=4)
• Mendeley (n=4)
• Espacenet (n=3)
0%
20%
40%
60%
80%
100%

FIGURE 47. Sources of metadata used to populate live RIM systems.

As to regional differences, the small sample for the US and Canada may suggest that the harvesting of PubMed content, mentioned by 73% of respondents and ranking first in that sub sample, is more relevant in these locales than in others. This would be plausible: PubMed is maintained by the US National Library of Medicine (NLM) with mirror sites in Europe and Canada, and it is a significant source for harvesting biomedical publications, particularly for institutions seeking to comply with US National Institutes of Health (NIH) Clinical and Translational Science Awards (CTSA) recommendations, calling for participating institutions to support collaboration among clinical and translational investigators through the provision of tools, training, and technology.[47] While the data does not robustly support this observation, it is one worth noting for potential closer investigation in future research.

RESEARCHER IDENTIFIERS

In this survey, respondents with live RIM system implementations were presented with eight researcher/person identifiers and five organizational identifiers and were asked which are currently used by their RIM system.

For researchers, the ORCID identifier is becoming a widespread, de facto standard within the RIM ecosystem, with 73% of respondents indicating their usage of ORCID iDs in their systems. Many institutions also report using the proprietary Scopus Author ID and ResearcherID to help disambiguate author names in the Scopus and Web of Science indexes, respectively, used to improve metadata harvesting at scale at many institutions.

ORCID adoption in RIM ecosystems was fairly consistent across geographic regions studied, although reported usage in Australia is lower (57%) than in other locales.

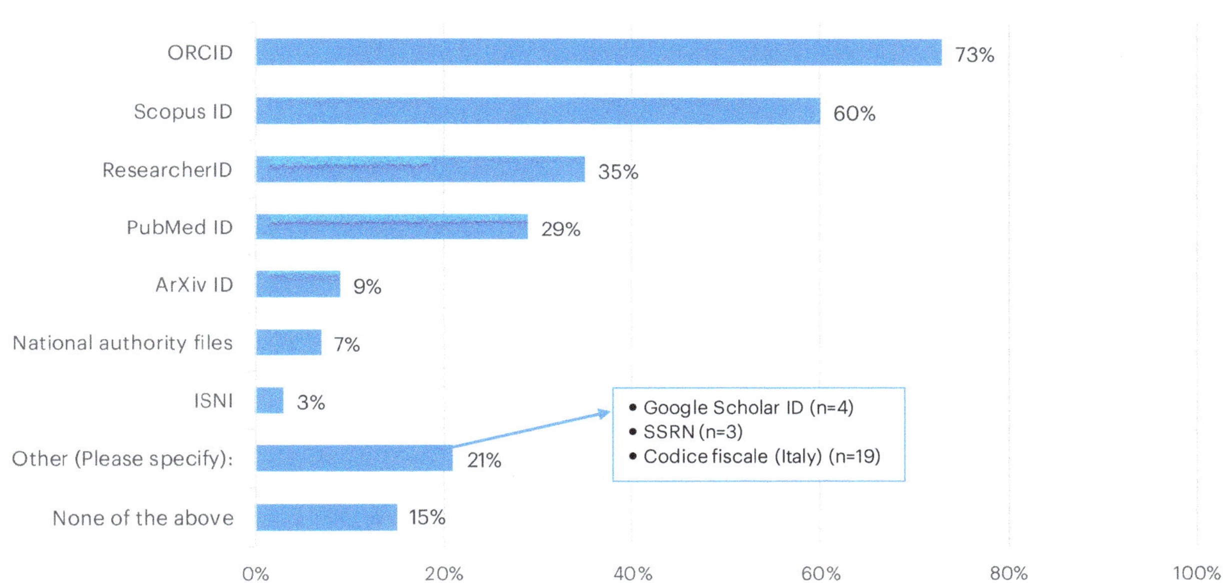
Researcher Identifiers Used in Your RIM system (n=182)
Note: Respondents could select more than one answer
ORCID
73%
Scopus ID
60%
ResearcherID
35%
PubMed ID
29%
ArXiv ID
9%
National authority files
7%
ISNI
3%
Other (Please specify):
21%
None of the above
15%
• Google Scholar ID (n=4)
• SSRN (n=3)
• Codice fiscale (Italy) (n=19)
0%
20%
40%
60%
80%
100%

FIGURE 48. Researcher and person identifiers in use in live RIM systems.

ORGANIZATIONAL IDENTIFIERS

While we observe that several person identifiers are being used in RIM systems across multiple countries, our survey indicates that there is little usage of organizational identifiers in RIM systems overall.

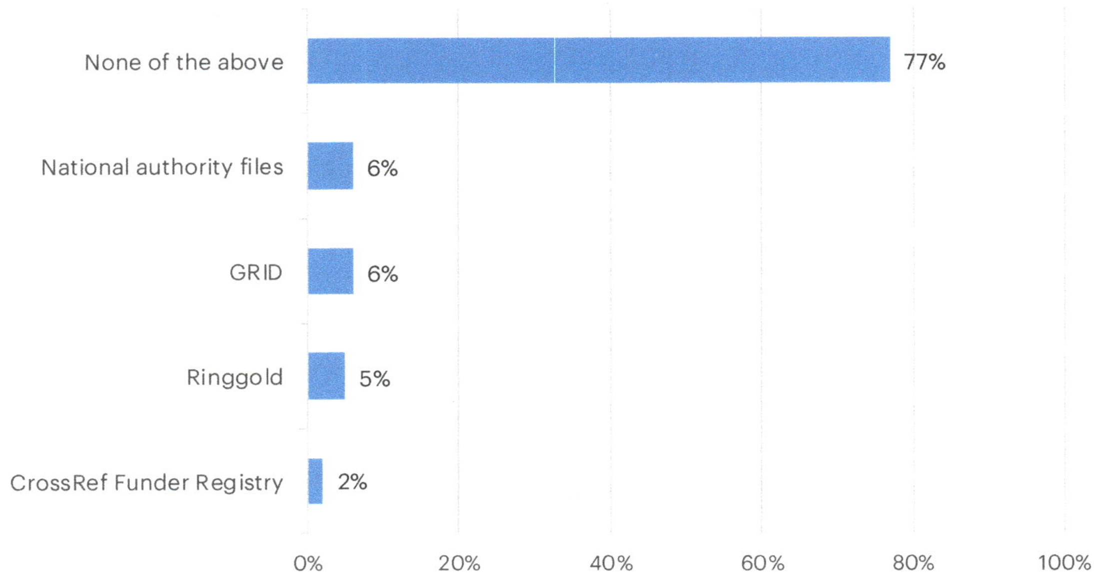
Organization Identifiers Used in Your RIM System (n=162)
Note: Respondents could select more than one answer
None of the above
77%
National authority files
6%
GRID
6%
Ringgold
5%
CrossRef Funder Registry
2%
0%
20%
40%
60%
80%
100%

FIGURE 49. Organizational identifiers in use in live RIM systems.

The response never topped 6% usage of any of the five organizational identifiers offered in the survey. Responses to this question do not negate the possibility that respondents may be using locally maintained organizational identifiers to manage their RIM work.

Our survey findings confirm and reinforce previous findings published in the 2017 OCLC Research Report *Convenience and Compliance: Case Studies on Persistent Identifiers in European Research Information*.[48] In that qualitative study, which examined RIM infrastructures and the adoption of persistent person and organizational identifiers in three European countries, Finland, Germany, and the Netherlands, the authors found widespread adoption of persistent person identifiers to support name disambiguation and improved publications metadata harvesting, and that ORCID is becoming the de facto standard for person identifiers. But while universities and ICT organizations are following international developments around organizational identifiers with interest, the authors observed no activities to integrate standardized organizational identifiers into RIM systems.

PROTOCOLS, STANDARDS, OR VOCABULARIES RIM SYSTEMS RELY ON

This section groups different protocols, standards, and vocabularies used by RIM systems in a single, rather diverse, category with the aim of assessing their adoption among institutions with live implementations as well as those currently implementing a RIM system. Respondents were allowed to select as many options as they saw fit.

It's unsurprising that 45% of both live and implementing institutions report using the OAI-PMH protocol, as just over half (54%) of survey respondents with live RIM systems indicated that their RIM serves as their default institutional repository. This suggests that these institutions are making sure the contents can be harvested by repository aggregators/harvesters like OpenAIRE, CORE, or the OCLC WorldCat OAIster, which rely upon the OAI-PMH protocol.[49]

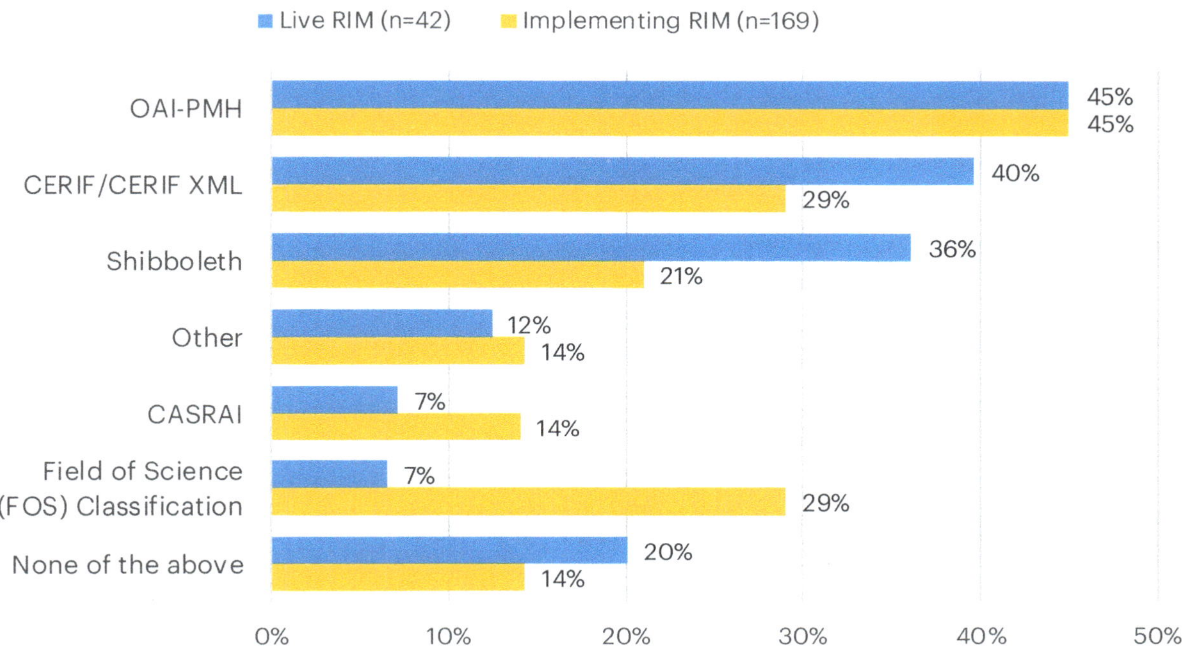

Protocols/Standards/Vocabularies that RIM Systems Rely On
Note: Respondents could select more than one answer
Live RIM (n=42)
Implementing RIM (n=169)
OAI-PMH
45%
45%
CERIF/CERIF XML
40%
29%
Shibboleth
36%
21%
Other
12%
14%
CASRAI
7%
14%
Field of Science (FOS) Classification
7%
29%
None of the above
20%
14%
0%
10%
20%
30%
40%
50%

FIGURE 50. Protocols, standards, and vocabularies in use for both live and implementing institutions.

The Common European Research Information Format (CERIF) is the second most popular protocol in use by survey respondents, with a 40% uptake across all respondents from institutions with a live RIM system, and 29% from institutions implementing one. Given that CERIF is the mechanism that ensures interoperability across systems (both at an institutional and at a national/regional or research funder level), a 40% uptake is significant. As a standard developed with the support of the European Commission and maintained by euroCRIS, it is unsurprising that among institutions with a live RIM system, CERIF usage is highest in Europe, with 57% of European institutions indicating they use this standard. Within the European sample, 70% of UK institutions report that CERIF is important, numbers likely driven by 2009 Jisc recommendations proposing the use of CERIF as the UK standard for research information exchange.[50] This is in sharp contrast to 9% in Australia and none in the US and Canada.

Thirty-six percent of institutions with live RIM systems and 21% of implementing institutions report using the Shibboleth protocol, reflecting the integration of RIM systems with authentication services—mainly at an institutional level. This is again an unsurprising result since 76% of institutions with live RIM systems report interoperability with an institutional authentication service such as Shibboleth. (See section on Internal and External Systems, page 74.)

Also relevant is the presence on the list, with a rather low level of adoption, of vocabularies related to research classifications. The use of standard vocabularies is recognized as important for system interoperability, but their adoption currently lags behind the adoption of some persistent identifiers and protocols. Stakeholders like CASRAI and euroCRIS are working on the gradual standardization Of this area, which should see significant progress in forthcoming years. The opportunity that this survey has provided for broadly capturing the current level of uptake for vocabularies like the OECD FOS classification, the Medical Subject Headings (MeSH) in the US or the Field of Research classification in Australia and New Zealand creates opportunities to revisit this question in a few years´ time to monitor progress. Inevitably, this area is also where the regional differences are bound to be more evident.[51]

SUMMARY: INTEROPERABILITY

> "We have three best of breed RIM systems that are interoperable to some extent, so we have as good a RIM infrastructure as is currently possible. The key to successful RIM going forward will be to improve and maximise interoperability." **(UK)**

System interoperability lies at the heart of research information management. **RIM implementations today feature integrations with an extensive number of internal and external systems**, and make use of a multitude of metadata sources for harvesting. Interoperability is regularly considered a key feature valued or desired in RIM systems, something expected to improve in future systems or configurations. The need for improved interoperability might even be shaping changes in product categories, as, e.g., RIM systems are sometimes used as scholarly communications repositories to alleviate interoperability problems upfront.

The use of identifiers, standards, and protocols in RIM fits into that pattern. **Adoption is strongest where the identifier or protocol in question also facilitates interoperability** and, more specifically, allows metadata harvesting or exchange, as ORCID, Scopus Author ID, and Researcher ID on the one hand and OAI-PMH on the other, do. CERIF as a European open standard information exchange format facilitating interoperability across systems is a notable regional example.

Interoperability between systems and data models helps reap the full benefits of RIM, but also remains a challenge, as respondents to this survey were eager to point out.

> "There is much room for improvement in the area of system interoperability. Only when such improvement takes place will the actual potential of RIM systems start to be realized." **(UK)**

CONCLUSION

> "The integration between the Research, Academic and Administrative processes is fundamental for the achievement of the institutional strategic objectives." **(translated from Spanish, Peru)**

> "RIM/CRIS in many institutions and countries are incredibly rich sources of research information, covering, combining and linking to each other all aspects of research (information): input (funding, capacity), project info, researcher info, publications, datasets, other results and products, equipment and services used, etc.. etc.. They represent a huge potential for the international community (not only the research community but also policy makers, and the public in general) when linked together into an international research information infrastructure. Not in the least for related research infrastructure initiatives such as the European Open Science Cloud." **(Netherlands)**

> "I am looking forward to the next generation of research management systems—everything currently on the market is built with old technology and old thinking—we need an apple I phone [sic] version of a research management system-intuitive, no training required, everything at your fingertips!" **(Australia)**

> "Needing to update outdated technology. A more integrated workflow and try to also make it more attractive to the Researcher and easier to use. The aim was to make it less manual." **(Australia)**

> "We highly believe in the 'one stop shop' for researchers regarding the information management of their research, including the archiving of research data. Furthermore [sic]: in a time of access 'by everyone to everything' (meaning specifically that a researcher can, uncontrolled, use a lot of applications, services, systems, etc.. 'out there' on the internet) we think it is very important for an institution/institute to have a cardinal source for accountability about the research executed by researchers appointed to that institution/institute. This source in our model is the RIM/CRIS. In other words: if the information is not in our RIM/CRIS it 'does not exist' for the institution/institute, no matter what a researcher/group states or mentions elsewhere, and the institution will only be accountable for the info in the RIM/CRIS. This is clearly communicated to our researchers." **(Netherlands)**

This 2017 RIM survey has been the largest and most comprehensive study ever conducted in the area of research information management practices. The overarching goal of this survey was to collect quantitative and qualitative data about research information management practices *worldwide*, and to provide a baseline of observations for future research. This survey has represented a significant strategic partnership between OCLC Research and euroCRIS, and our organizations plan to repeat this survey in future years, developing longitudinal data and knowledge about evolving practices in order to inform the research community about the changing goals, purposes, and scope of RIM practices. We also hope that our research efforts will inspire complementary research efforts at a national or regional level, where there are more uniform open science and research assessment policies and frameworks.

Current RIM practices reveal an extensive range of platforms and configurations to support institutional and researcher needs. Increasingly consolidated commercial and open-source platforms are becoming widely implemented across regions, coexisting with a large number of region-specific solutions. However, this survey has also revealed that locally developed systems still play an important role.

Research information management practices are complex, and institutions frequently report using several systems to support research information workflows that increasingly demand greater interoperability—with both internal and external systems. The range of system configurations that institutions use to implement a RIM strategy is far wider than the operation of a specific platform, and it's common to see institutions running an array of interconnected systems to cover an increasing number of objectives. Interoperability is regularly considered a key feature valued or desired in a RIM system, something expected to improve in future systems or configurations, and the use of identifiers, standards, and protocols are perceived as most valuable when they can also facilitate interoperability. The need for improved interoperability is likely also driving the increasing functional merging of RIM systems and institutional repositories observed in this survey.

The range of system configurations that institutions use to implement a RIM strategy is far wider than the operation of a specific platform

This survey has also documented the complex, cross-stakeholder teams needed to work together to provide the best possible research support service. While the research office was reported as a leading stakeholder in RIM practices, the library was also shown to have significant responsibilities, particularly related to support for open access, copyright, and deposit; metadata entry and validation; training and support; and research data management. Survey responses further emphasized that these library interactions were often related to the library's responsibility for one or more scholarly communications repositories, and reinforce the increasing overlap of practice and workflows between previously siloed RIM systems and repository systems.

By examining research information practices from a global perspective, we are better able to understand the importance and breadth of national research assessment frameworks and open science policies as key drivers strongly shaping priorities of RIM activities in those countries and regions where they exist. There is an emerging set of additional objectives—such as the need to improve services for researchers or the need to support institutional reputation and decision-making—that institutions operating in less demanding policy environments see as key incentives for their own RIM strategies.

This report has frequently emphasized the analysis of regional differences in order to provide insights on the variations in practices and their level of consolidation. It will be informative to repeat the survey in a few years' time to see how the ecosystems change and evolve, as policies become more homogenous across regions, or if RIM practices develop along different lines from the ones adopted by the early implementers.

Areas for future research

Finding the right audience for this survey has been a significant challenge. The stakeholder analysis has confirmed how vital a role the research office plays in research information management, as well as the increasing engagement of libraries in the RIM space. This might come as a surprise for those who think of RIM from a purely administrative perspective; publications on the research information and management landscape frequently do not say much about libraries,[52] and research administrators often are unaware of library work and expertise and how it overlaps with and complements their own. **Research information management requires cross-functional, enterprise wide relationships**, but institutional stakeholders may lack optimal knowledge or connections. Future research efforts might investigate or help alleviate this disconnect, and bring multiple stakeholder perspectives to the table, in concert, when examining RIM practices.

The survey revealed some potential trends that merit follow-up in their own right or because of our inability to complete adequate analysis due to small sample sizes. For example, we observed RIM adoption growing in countries without strong national reporting mandates, driven by reasons other than compliance, such as improved decision support and improved researcher services. If true, this could shape the landscape of RIM considerably, feature and solution wise, and be of additional benefit to established adopters of RIM systems.

In the same context, it will be worthwhile to observe longitudinally how the need to track usage of research facilities and equipment becomes a more important component of RIM activities as institutions begin to link and evaluate research projects and outcomes with means, including grants and funding but also material or logistical support of the research effort.

Equally, the role of research data management as part of RIM is still evolving and an area worth watching, regarding system support and workflow integration with RIM, a development potentially led by Europe. The gradual merging of RIM and IR functional categories we observed warrants dedicated attention in future research.

Finally, reviewing and comparing levels of adoption, with regional distinctions, for standard vocabularies facilitating interoperability will be an opportunity to follow-up on in the future.

Concerning regional differences, the United States has often been a "plausible outlier" in our comparisons. Given the lack of mandates for institutions to track and report on levels of open access, as well as the absence of any national research assessment program, US responses often stand in stark contrast to others regarding the perceived value of RIM functions supporting compliance such as the registration of research outputs. The comparatively stronger role that researcher expertise discovery plays in driving RIM practices in the US—and that we suspect to be much stronger even than we can demonstrate here—also stands out, just like the comparatively stronger role of PubMed harvesting compared to other content sources, probably driven by compliance with US National Institutes of Health (NIH) Clinical and Translational Science Awards (CTSA) recommendations. In this survey, we often saw assumptions confirmed, without being able to robustly underpin them with quantitative data, due to sample size. This is definitely something we are eager to improve on in a future edition of this survey.

Overall, future research might be able to sketch a richer and more diversified RIM landscape including systems and communities focusing on researcher profiles, such as Profiles RNS and VIVO, grant management systems, research administration systems, and other systems covering established or emerging parts of RIM. Region-specific systems not well known outside their market but complementing the landscape for the institutions concerned deserve more attention. Not least, analysis will greatly benefit from a stronger reference to the many national or regional scale efforts in the space, at the system, data, or services level, and a stronger matching of RIM incentives to the specific policy landscape they are shaped by.

ACKNOWLEDGMENTS

This survey and report represent a significant community effort. While those of us who have expended sustained, considerable effort in preparing, administering, analyzing, and writing this report are named as co-authors, we wish to acknowledge the contributions of many others who have helped to bring this report to fruition.

Julie Griffin, Associate Dean of Research and Informatics at Virginia Tech University; Constance Malpas, former Strategic Intelligence Manager & Research Scientist at OCLC; and Rachael Samberg, Scholarly Communication Officer at the University of California, Berkeley, were all early and important contributors as we designed the survey instrument. Muhammed Javed (Cornell University) and Maliaca Oxnam (University of Arizona) joined our working group during the synthesis and writing stage, offering much-appreciated edits and insights.

Many members of the OCLC Research Library Partnership and euroCRIS communities also supported us by beta testing the survey instrument, including:

- Carol Feltes, The Rockefeller University
- Bob Gerrity, The University of Queensland
- Paolo Mangiafico, Duke University
- Valerie McCutcheon, University of Glasgow
- Kevin Miller, University of California, Davis
- César Olivares, CONCYTEC
- Jordan Piščanc, University of Trieste
- Birgit Schmidt, Göttingen State and University Library
- Ed Simons, Radboud University and euroCRIS
- Karen Smith-Yoshimura, OCLC Research
- Karla Strieb, The Ohio State University

We could not have implemented or analyzed this survey without the outstanding efforts of the market analysis team at OCLC, including Janet Hawk, Peggy Gallagher, and Joanne Cantrell. They improved the survey instrument by enhancing and adding questions, created the online survey instrument and necessary logic, supported the survey implementation, and delivered a robust initial analysis and dataset to the survey working group. They also provided us with valuable guidance to be in compliance with new GDPR requirements. Christopher Cyr in OCLC Research has also provided additional data analysis expertise when we encountered data complexities. Finally, the report couldn't have been published without the significant efforts of the OCLC Research publishing team, including Erin M. Schadt, Jeannette McNicol, and JD Shipengrover.

Ultimately, this survey—and future surveys that will enable us to develop longitudinal data about research information management practices worldwide—was made possible by the senior leadership of OCLC and euroCRIS. We wish to particularly thank Lorcan Dempsey, Vice President, Membership and Research, Chief Strategist of OCLC and Ed Simons, President, euroCRIS, for their sustained support of this effort.

NOTES

1. euroCRIS: Current Research Information Systems. "Main Features of CERIF." http://www.eurocris.org/cerif/main-features-cerif; OCLC Research. "About." https://www.oclc.org/research/about.html.

2. "OCLC Research and euroCRIS Announce Strategic Partnership." Posted 18 October 2017. https://www.oclc.org/en/news/releases/2017/201728dublin.html.

3. Ribeiro, Lígia, Pablo De Castro, and Michele Mennielli. 2016. *EUNIS-EuroCRIS Joint Survey on CRIS and IR*. Final Report. http://www.eurocris.org/news/cris-ir-survey-report.

4. Bryant, Rebecca, Anna Clements, Carol Feltes, David Groenewegen, Simon Huggard, Holly Mercer, Roxanne Missingham, Maliaca Oxnam, Anne Rauh and John Wright. 2017. *Research Information Management: Defining RIM and the Library's Role*. Dublin, OH: OCLC Research. https://doi:10.25333/C3NK88.

5. Ibid., 6.

6. Ribeiro, Castro, and Mennielli, *EUNIS-EuroCRIS Joint Survey*, 11 (see note 3).

7. Science Europe. 2016. "Science Europe Position Statement on Research Information Systems." https://doi:D/2016/13.324/11.

8. Dempsey, Lorcan. 2014. Research Information Management Systems – A New Service Category? *Lorcan Dempsey's Weblog*. 26 October 2014. http://orweblog.oclc.org/research-information-management-systems-a-new-service-category/.

9. Sivertsen, Gunnar. 2017. "Unique, but Still Best Practice? The Research Excellence Framework (REF) from an International Perspective." *Palgrave Communications* 3, no. 17078 (August 2017). https://doi.org/10.1057/palcomms.2017.78.

10. See the distribution of open access policies by policy maker type at University of Southampton's ROARMAP Registry of Open Access Repository Madates and Policies database: http://roarmap.eprints.org/view/policymaker_type/.

11. For instance, the Dutch roadmap aims for 60% open access by 2018 and 100% by 2024. See the VSNU report, "The Netherlands: Paving the Way for Open Access." http://vsnu.nl/files/documenten/Domeinen/Onderzoek/Open%20access/Ezine-OpenAccess-ENG-mrch2016.pdf.

12. UK Research and Innovation, "Open Access Policy," https://www.ukri.org/funging/information-for-award-holders/open-access/open-access-policy/ [formerly Research Councils UK; archives available at The National Archives: https://webarchive.nationalarchives.gov.uk/*/http:/www.rcuk.ac.uk/];

    Australian Government 2018. *National Health and Medical Research Council Open Access Policy*. [Sydney], Australia: NHMRC. https://nhmrc.gov.au/about-us/publications/open-access-policy [downloadable pdf];

    Australian Research Council (ARC). "Open Access Policy." http://www.arc.gov.au/arc-open-access-policy;

Page, Benedict. 2016. "EU Sets 2020 Target for Open Access Science Research." *The Bookseller*. (News). Published 31 May 2016. https://www.thebookseller.com/news/eu-all-scientific-articles-must-be-open-access-2020-330711;

Matthews, David. 2018. "Europe Set to Miss Flagship Open Access Target." *Times Higher Education*. (News) Published 7 March 2018. https://www.timeshighereducation.com/news/europe-set-miss-flagship-open-access-target. [requires login; free registration];

Swan, Alma, Yassine Gargouri, Megan Hunt, and Stevan Harnad. 2015. *Working Together to Promote Open Access Policy Alignment in Europe—Work Package 3 Report: Open Access Policies*. Luxembourg: European Commission, EKT/NHRF. http://www.pasteur4oa.eu/sites/pasteur4oa/files/deliverables/PASTEUR4OA Work Package 3 Report final 10 March 2015.pdf; and

The Registry of Open Access Repository Mandates and Policies (ROARMAP) maintains a database of these policies, https://roarmap.eprints.org/.

13. The European Open Science Cloud (EOSC)s an example of this type of practice on a large scale, https://ec.europa.eu/research/openscience/index.cfm?pg=open-science-cloud.

14. Ribeiro, Lígia, Pablo De Castro, and Michele Mennielli. 2016. *EUNIS-EuroCRIS Joint Survey on CRIS and IR*. Final Report. http://www.eurocris.org/news/cris-ir-survey-report; Sticht, Kendra. 2015. "Ergebnisbericht Einsatz von Forschungsinformationssystemen an Universitäten Und Hochschulen Mit Promotionsrecht in Deutschland (Use of Research Information Systems at Universities and Colleges with Doctoral Rights in Germany. Score Report)," https://doi.org/10.5281/zenodo.15590.

15. Survey dataset: https://doi.org/10.25333/QXR6-D439.

16. EU General Data Protection Regulation (GDPR): https://www.eugdpr.org/.

17. Melgar-Sasieta, Hector-Andres, Ian-Paul Brossard-Nunez, and Cesar-Augusto Olivares-Poggi. 2018. "Current Status of Research Information Management in Peru." Presentation delivered at the CRIS2018 Conference Umeå within parallel session 5 "Policy and Assessment", 13-16 June, 2018. http://hdl.handle.net/11366/672.

18. Bryant, Rebecca. 2017. "Announcing a Spanish Language Version of the Survey on Research Information Management Practices," *HangingTogether* (blog), *OCLC Research*. 26 November 2017. http://hangingtogether.org/?p=6350.

19. The Peruvian National Council for Science, Technology, and Innovation held the first Peruvian National Conference on Research Information Management on 19-20 July 2018 at the Catholic University Santa María in Arequipa, Peru, and preliminary findings from this survey were presented at that event. See de Castro, Pablo. 2018. "First Peruvian National Conference on Research Information Management," *euroCRIS Blog*. 30 July 2018, https://www.eurocris.org/blog/first-peruvian-national-conference-research-information-management.

20. Mike Conlon, VIVO Project Leader, reported via personal communication to Muhammad Javed on 20 July 2018 that there are currently 158 VIVO installations, including 93 in the US. We had only eight VIVO institutions participate in the survey.

21. For example, one respondent informed us that "(we have a separate grants management system – this survey is only being answered for our publications/research activities system)."

22. Germany-based Avedas was acquired by Thomson Reuters in 2013. See Gfii Groupement Français de l'Industrie de l'Information. "Thomson Reuters Acquires AVEDAS and Expands Its Scholarly-Research Analytics Solution." 2013. http://www.gfii.fr/en/document/thomson-reuters-acquires-avedas-and-expands-its-scholarly-research-analytics-solution; DSpace-CRIS was developed and maintained in Italy with funding from Hong Kong University and OpenAire. See DuraSpace. "DSpace-CRIS Home." https://wiki.duraspace.org/display/DSPACECRIS/DSpace-CRIS+Home.

23. Cineca. "IRIS - International Research Information System." https://www.cineca.it/en/content/iris-institutional-research-information-system.

24. infoEd Global: Research Administration Without Boundaries, Research Without Boundarlies. http://infoedglobal.com.

25. Database Consultants Australia (DCA), ResearchMaster: https://www.researchmaster.com.au/.

26. OMEGA-PSIR Scientific Information System: http://en.omegapsir.io/.

27. The full list of verbatim responses for this and other sections can be found in the accompanying supplemental materials.

28. U-GOV Ricerca and Metis were previously widely used in Italy and the Netherlands, respectively. https://www.cineca.it/it/content/u-gov-ricerca; euroCRIS, Research Object METIS Research Information System: https://dspacecris.eurocris.org/cris/dris/dris00902.

29. See for instance these recent "case studies for sharing research equipment" by the Jisc-funded equipment.data project in the UK, https://equipment.jiscinvolve.org/wp/.

30. Harvard Catalyst, Harvard Catalyst Profiles: https://connects.catalyst.harvard.edu/.

31. Established in 2007, the National Academic Research and Collaborations Information System (NARCIS: https://www.narcis.nl/) is a national Dutch portal that combines data from three heterogeneous and independently managed types of sources: Institutional CRIS systems, aggregated in NOD (the Dutch Research Database); Digital academic repositories; and research data sets, including those from the 4TU archive and in the DANS-EASY archive. NARCIS aggregates content and provides discovery and access to scientific research, including nearly 500,000 open-access publications and datasets, from all Dutch universities, several research institutes, KNAW, and NWO. See also Bryant, Rebecca, Annette Dortmund, and Constance Malpas. 2017. *Convenience and Compliance: Case Studies on Persistent Identifiers in European Research Information, 8* Dublin, Ohio: OCLC Research. https://doi:10.25333/C32K7.

32. Awards management workflows are closely integrated with other RIM functionalities in some locales, such as the myResearch workflows at Monash University in Australia. See Monash University. 2016 "myResearch Enters Next Phase." *News & Events*. Posted 1 June 2016. http://www.monash.edu/news/articles/myresearch-enters-next-phase.

33. National mandates in the UK (Research Excellence Framework, or REF) and Australia (Excellence for Research, or ERA) require institutions to collect research outputs and measure the impact of sponsored research.

34. Stebbins, Michael. 2013. "Expanding Public Access to the Results of Federally Funded Research." *What's Happening* (blog). *the White House: President Barack Obama*. 22 February 2018. https://obamawhitehouse.archives.gov/blog/2013/02/22/expanding-public-access-results-federally-funded-research.

35. Bryant, Dortmund, and Malpas. *Convenience and Compliance (see note 31).*

36. de Castro, Pablo, Kathleen Shearer, and Friedrich Summann. 2014. "The Gradual Merging of Repository and CRIS Solutions to Meet Institutional Research Information Management Requirements," 40. *Procedia Computer Science* 33 (January): 39–46. https://doi:10.1016/J.PROCS.2014.06.007.

37. Ribeiro, Castro, and Mennielli, *EUNIS-EuroCRIS Joint Survey*, 10 (see note 3).

38. Coalition for Networked Information (CNI). 2017. *Rethinking Institutional Repository Strategies: Report of a CNI Executive Roundtable*. Washington, D.C.: Coalition for Networked Information. https://www.cni.org/wp-content/uploads/2017/05/CNI-rethinking-irs-exec-rndtbl.report.S17.v1.pdf.

39. Ribeiro, Castro, and Mennielli, *EUNIS-EuroCRIS Joint Survey*, 18 (see note 3).

40. De Castro, Shearer, and Summann, "Gradual Merging," (see note 36).

41. One acknowledged limitation of this sample is the n=0 representation by institutions in Norway, compared to n=16 sample in the euroCRIS-EUNIS survey. Norway has a national adopted CRIS system (CRIStin), well-integrated with local repositories, and particularly supporting ETD repository integration.

42. We also want to point out that service providers like Elsevier and Digital Science are positioning themselves with product offerings in multiple categories, including RIM and repository classes, which may represent positioning to optimize integration, market share, and potential revenues as the need for interoperability increases. See particularly, "Elsevier Acquires Bepress, A Leading Service Provider Used by Academic Institutions to Showcase their Research." 2017. Posted 2 August 2017. https://www.elsevier.com/about/press-releases/corporate/elsevier-acquires-bepress,-a-leading-service-provider-used-by-academic-institutions-to-showcase-their-research; and https://www.digital-science.com/.

43. Eight of 12 Dutch research universities are included in this sample.

44. For instance: Anderson, Jan, Kristel Toom, Susi Poli, and Pamela F. Miller. 2018. Research Management: Europe and Beyond. London, UK: Academic Press.

45. These are also elements congruent with the description of the library's role in RIM articulated in the OCLC Research position paper. See Bryant et al. *Defining RIM,* 12-15 (see note 4).

46. Ibid., 12-15.

47. Harvard Catalyst. "About." https://catalyst.harvard.edu/about/.

48. Bryant, Dortmund, and Malpas. *Convenience and Compliance (see note 31).*

49. OpenAire. https://www.openaire.eu/; Core. "Aggregating the World's Open Access Research Papers." https://core.ac.uk/; OCLC. "The OAIster database." https://www.oclc.org/en/oaister.html.

50. Wilsdon, James, Liz Allen, Eleonora Belfiore, Philip Campbell, Stephen Curry, Steven Hill, Richard Jones, Roger Kain, Simon Kerridge, Mike Thelwall, Jane Tinkler, Ian Viney, Paul Wouters, Jude Hill, and Ben Johnson. 2015. *The Metric Tide: Report of the Independent Review of the Role of Metrics in Research Assessment and Management, 20.* https://doi.org/10.13140/RG.2.1.4929.1363. [Today the majority of RIM systems in use in the UK are CERIF compliant]

51. casrai. "Research Classification." http://dictionary.casrai.org/Research_Classification; NIH: U.S. National Library of Medicine. "Medical Subject Headings." https://www.nlm.nih.gov/mesh/; Wikipedia. "Fields of Science and Technology." https://en.wikipedia.org/wiki/Fields_of_Science_and_Technology; University of South Australia. "Development and Management of Research Projects." http://w3.unisa.edu.au/res/admin/for.asp.

52. Anderson et al. *Europe and Beyond* (see note 44).

For more information about our work on research information management, please visit: **oc.lc/rim**

OCLC

6565 Kilgour Place
Dublin, Ohio 43017-3395

T: 1-800-848-5878
T: +1-614-764-6000
F: +1-614-764-6096
www.oclc.org/research

ISBN: 978-1-55653-073-9
DOI: 10.25333/bgfg-d241
RM-PR-216156-WWAE 1812

www.ingramcontent.com/pod-product-compliance
Lightning Source LLC
Chambersburg PA
CBHW041431270326
41934CB00022B/3498
9781556530739